# Deliverance From Addiction

## Breaking the Yoke & Healing the Hurt

Thomas W. Pohl

Written Words Publishing LLC
P.O. Box 462622
Aurora, Colorado 80046
www.writtenwordspublishing.com

Published by Written Words Publishing LLC December 20, 2024

ISBN: 978-1-961610-24-8 (paperback)
ISBN: 978-1-961610-25-5 (eBook)

Library of Congress Control Number: 2024924941

Cover designed by Written Words Publishing LLC

Manufactured and printed in the United States of America

# DEDICATION

This book is lovingly dedicated to our Lord and Savior Jesus Christ without whom this book would not be possible. I pray that everyone who reads this book will be blessed by it, and those of you suffering from the yoke of drug addiction will be delivered from it by the power of Jesus Christ. God bless you all!

# In Loving Memory

of

Jessica

*"Until we meet again, Sunshine."*

# TABLE OF CONTENTS

# PREFACE

I never thought I would write this book. In fact, I was in the middle of writing another book when the Lord dropped this one on me. I thought I was done with the whole "drug world" after my dear friend Marie died of complications from an overdose. I struggled and procrastinated with writing this book because, in reality, I wasn't interested in the subject matter nor did I want to be involved in the "drug world" anymore. Although her death pained me greatly, it also brought a sense of liberty and relieved me from having to deal with that stuff. However, every time I fought against writing this book, the Holy Spirit brought to my remembrance a quote by Terri Savelle Foy, a noted Christian minister, "Someone is waiting on the other side of your obedience." If God has given me this assignment, He obviously knows it will help and be a blessing to someone.

Two years later, when this book was nearly finished, I was at Bible Study one evening when the Holy Spirit reminded me that shortly after Marie had passed away, and in the midst of my pain, I had pleaded with God and said, "Don't let her death be in vain! Turn this around for good!" He then said, "That book was the answer to your plea." This gave me a new conviction to get it finished and published.

I hope this book will be both educational and a blessing to you, whether you are struggling with drug addiction or you are someone who loves a person who is.

# INTRODUCTION

Addiction ensnares all kinds of individuals. It doesn't care about one's circumstances, title, position in life, or whether they are a good person or not. I've known individuals who fit in all these categories and became addicts. Most of the addicts I've known did not choose to use drugs initially. I don't know of a single person who woke up one morning and said, "Hmm, I think I'll try heroin today."

I was never the type of person who would be interested in using illegal drugs. When I was a teenager, I joked that I wouldn't know where to get them, even if I wanted them. I was pretty much oblivious to that world until December 2014, when God introduced me to my best friend, Ashley, who was a hardcore drug addict. She also had two sisters who struggled with drug addiction, but Ashley's addiction was the worst of the three by far. In the ensuing years, I would learn that several other members of her family were drug addicts as well. My experiences with her and her family have helped to shape a great deal of the content contained in this book.

The main purpose of *Deliverance From Addiction* is to dispel the prevailing narrative that drug addiction is an incurable brain disease, which can only be managed. I have seen firsthand that this is simply not true. Drug addiction is more like being in bondage.

Throughout this book, I will demonstrate how to separate the person from their addiction because the addiction does not define who the person really is. The stories are about real people. We should recognize that 'real people' have 'real challenges.' Do not feel sorry for the individuals but develop 'empathy' for them as they struggle with bondage.

*Deliverance From Addiction* encompasses what I've learned about drug addiction, drug addicts, conquering addiction, and the revelation God has given me. I use the overarching term "drugs" to indicate both the illegal variety and prescription medication that is often abused.

# PART I: AN INTRODUCTION TO DRUG ADDICTION

## CHAPTER ONE

## SHUNNING THE DRUG ADDICT

Initially, when I started hanging out with Ashley, my family thought I was crazy. My cousin Liz admonished me like I was one of her children and said, "Stay the fuck away from Ashley. She's a drug addict and a known prostitute." I responded, "Don't worry. I know what I'm doing." I don't blame Liz for her concern. She was worried Ashley would drag me down to her level. Instead, over the next four years, I pulled Ashley up out of the gutter again and again until the black hole of drug addiction finally lost its grip on her. Family members and co-workers constantly told me things like "Get rid of her," "She's sucking you dry," "She's going to crash your car," and a myriad of other derogatory comments. In the end, I proved them all wrong, and so did Ashley.

One day, I said to Liz, "Remember when I first started hanging out with Ashley and you told me to stay away from her?"

Liz replied, "Yeah."

I then stated, "Aren't you glad I didn't listen to you?"

Liz emphatically said, "Yeah." She had witnessed Ashley's transformation over those four years and acknowledged the positive change in her and in her life.

I said, "See, I told you I knew what I was doing."

Liz and others had automatically shunned Ashley because she was a drug addict. Unfortunately, shunning is the prevailing attitude of society towards individuals who are addicted to drugs. There is a negative stigma attached to those who use drugs on a regular basis. It doesn't matter whether they want to be free from their addiction but can't get free, or if they like doing drugs and aren't interested in getting clean, or if they see nothing wrong with using a particular drug (like Millennials who use marijuana, for example). Generally, drug addicts are treated like lepers were in biblical times—as unclean and societal outcasts. They are seen as low lives and losers who are often classified as morally corrupt individuals. People assume they have mental issues. Their relatives usually do not acknowledge them because of the shame they would bring on the family. They are frequently treated as the black sheep that no one wants around or to be around.

Drug addicts are usually shunned by society because of the negative behaviors drug addicts tend to display toward others. Are all drug addicts scumbags? Not necessarily. Do they engage in scumbag-type behavior? Absolutely! However, their negative behavior is generally a by-product of their addiction, which was manifested in the addict's quest to acquire the resources needed to feed their addiction. Such actions often cause conflict between the addict and those around them, especially if they are the victims of the addict's bad conduct. In addition, it also creates a great deal of stress for those who are forced to deal with the addict.

Drug addiction is stigmatized worse than mental illness by many individuals. Some even view it as incurable. In later chapters, we will see that drug addiction is indeed conquerable.

# PART II: How and Why People Get Addicted

## Chapter Two

## How People Get Addicted

To understand how people succumb to the yoke of drug addiction, it is necessary to examine the many factors that ensnare individuals into drug addiction. Some factors that can lead to drug addiction include a person's current or past living environment, family history of addiction, the people they hang out with, the places they frequent, dependence on medication that was prescribed for legitimate needs, and unresolved trauma in the individual's past. Let us examine these factors in more detail.

### Living Environment

An individual's living environment, either past or current, can have a big impact on whether they may get trapped by drug addiction. If a person grew up in a household where other family members were drug users, the chances that they themselves will try drugs is greatly increased, especially if the use of drugs within the household is seen as "normal" to them. At times, the individual allows themselves to be influenced and/or peer pressured by their family members. I have known people who grew up in or lived in toxic households who later experimented with drugs and/or became addicts.

## Family History

Family history of drug addiction can play a huge part in the likelihood of a person becoming addicted. From my observations, addiction tends to run in families. I know three sisters who suffered from drug addiction. Their mother became addicted to drugs after getting hooked on pain medication and died of an overdose. Their father was a compulsive gambling addict. I also know another mother and daughter and a mother and son who all suffered from drug addiction. They were members of the same extended family.

## People

The people one hangs out with can have a big influence on a person's decision to try drugs and ultimately become addicted. I have learned from my own personal experience that people have a tendency to act like those they spend recreational time with. This can be both positive and negative. Jim Rohn, a noted motivational speaker, famously said, "You are the average of the five people you spend the most time with."

We should pay close attention to who we are spending time with the most and never underestimate the influence of our peers. An example of this includes a friend who got addicted because she often socialized with her mother who was a drug addict and actually gave her daughter crack at the age of 15. The two of them would often hang out with other drugs users as well. Because of the tendency for drug addicts to be shunned by others, the only people willing to be around them are usually other addicts.

Another example is when a friend who was a drug addict dated another drug addict for a year and a half and he dragged her deeper into addiction than she had been previously. The good news is that once he was out of her life and she continued to be around people who were a positive influence on her, she got clean two months later and accepted Jesus Christ as her Lord and Savior.

I can also testify to being influenced by others. Early in my Christian walk, I began to notice that when I hung out with my non-Christian friends, I tended to act like them. Conversely, when I was around my Christian friends, I mimicked their behavior.

Who is in our circle matters and there is nothing wrong with having a small circle.

## Places

The places where people gather can have an influence on their behavior. If an individual frequently hangs out in places where drug use is common, the likelihood of them trying drugs is increased, especially if they are the type of person who is easily influenced. This goes hand in hand with the people one surrounds themselves with. This is why drug rehabilitation centers emphasize to those in their care to stay away from people, places and things that are triggers for their addiction.

## Prescription Medication

Being addicted to prescription medication has become more common in recent years. Doctors tend to overprescribe medication. It is their first go-to, usually because drug companies pay doctors to push their pills. The two most common types of prescription medication that individuals get addicted to are opiate pain medication and benzodiazepines.

Examples of opiate pain medication include Oxycodone, Roxicodone, Hydrocodone, Morphine, Codeine, Methadone, Percocet, and others. Examples of benzodiazepines include Xanax, Klonopin, Valium, Ativan, and others. While many individuals start taking these medications for legitimate health and/or mental health needs, all too often they wind up getting addicted. This is especially true if the individual has any of the above risk factors present in their life.

I have a friend with a family history of drug addiction who was prescribed opiate pain medication for a back injury she suffered from a car accident. She soon became addicted and kept getting refill prescriptions. When her doctor would no longer prescribe them, she went "doctor shopping" to find one who would. When that option finally ran out and she was desperate, a so-called "friend" suggested she try heroin. This resulted in her being consumed by drug addiction for many years. She proceeded to use other hardcore drugs, like cocaine and crack. She abused other prescription medications as well, particularly Xanax. Fortunately, she conquered her addiction through her faith in Jesus.

Another friend of mine suffered between bouts of drug addiction and being clean. She did well staying clean until she was in a car accident and was prescribed opiate pain medication. Given her past history of opiate addiction, she quickly became addicted again. She went on to use harder illegal opiates, including Heroin and Fentanyl. She was desperate to be free from her addiction, which she admitted she allowed to get out of control by her own choices, but she did not know how.

A former co-worker became addicted to opiate pain medication that was prescribed because of back issues he suffered. This man was a deacon at his local church, yet he still got addicted! Addiction doesn't care about a person's status or title; it can ensnare anyone. Fortunately, he did not have a history of drug addiction and was able to successfully kick the habit after going to a drug rehabilitation facility.

# CHAPTER THREE

# DRUGS AND TRAUMA

Trauma is one of the most common and damaging factors that can lead to drug addiction. It can be physical, mental, emotional, or sexual. Trauma can cause people to suffer from depression, anxiety, grief, poor relationships, risky behavior, and even suicidal tendencies. Often, these factors will cause a person to want to numb themselves to their pain by using drugs, which ultimately becomes a coping mechanism for many of these individuals. For one reason or another, they tend to avoid dealing with the root causes of their trauma. Most of the drug addicts I have met have some form of unresolved trauma in their past. Some have successfully dealt with it, but most have not.

One of the most outspoken proponents of the correlation between addiction and trauma is Dr. Gabor Maté. He is a renowned speaker and bestselling author who is highly sought after for his expertise on a range of topics including addiction and childhood development. According to his expertise, addiction is the result of trauma. He has publicly stated, "Addiction is not a choice. It's not a moral failure. It's not an ethical lapse. It's not a weakness of character. It's not a failure of will. It's not how society depicts addiction, nor is it an inherited brain disease, which is the medical tendency to see it. But what it is, actually is, is a response to human suffering."

He also said, "All these children I have worked with have been severely traumatized as children. All the women had been sexually abused. All the men had been traumatized.

Some of them sexually, physically, emotionally neglected." Contrary to what medical professionals say, addiction is "actually an attempt to escape suffering, temporarily."

Concerning the media's depiction of addiction, Dr. Maté said, "The media, the television, cultural depiction of addiction is showing desperate people without showing why they are desperate. All they show is that desperation for the drug. There is no indication what is driving that desperation. And as you see them behaving in all kinds of dysfunctional ways, aggressive, manipulative, unpleasant, there is no three-dimensional sense of reality about these people."

He also said, "What you have is traumatized children. When children are traumatized, it affects how they feel about themselves, which is deeply ashamed. If a child believes it is all about themselves, they must be a terrible person, or if I was sexually abused, 'Why didn't I fight back. I must be a very weak person.' So, there's a deep sense of shame. Then there's tremendous emotional pain that accrues from abuse and neglect. Tremendous emotional pain that is hardly possible for people to bear. They have to soothe their pain with substances. Then the trauma, given that the human brain develops an interaction with the environment, shapes the brain's circuitry in such a way that the person may be more likely to find relief from the drugs. The very physiology of the brain is affected by early trauma."

In regards to society's response to drug use, Dr. Maté stated, "Then you take these traumatized people, make their habit illegal. It's not illegal to drink yourself to death. It's not illegal to make yourself sick with emphysema or lung cancer by means of cigarettes, but it's illegal to use other substances. So now you take these abused, traumatized people, and put them outside the law. You put them in jail, you hound them all their lives. You treat them like criminals and bad people and failures and rejects and wonder how come they don't get better. So, it's a self-perpetuating cycle of taking traumatized people and retraumatizing them, and then hoping at the same time why don't they listen, why don't they get better already, why don't they give it up. They don't give it up because the more they hurt, the more they need to escape. So, the addiction was really an attempt to solve the problem. If you ask, 'Why do people use substances or why do they engage in addiction in general?' It's because they have a problem they don't know what to do with."

Then the question needs to be asked, "'What gave you such emotional pain and how come you didn't have the internal resources?' It's not a judgement, it's simply just an inquiry. How can you lack at some point the internal resources to deal with that pain in a more creative, forward-looking way that would help you resolve the pain than to perpetuate it? What really happened was the addiction came along to help you solve a problem you had no other solutions for at the time and that's the case for all addictions."[1]

> *"Trauma creates change you don't choose. Healing is about creating change you do choose."* – Michelle Rosenthal

Healing from trauma will help an individual overcome drug addiction. One of the most important things a person can do to progress towards their freedom from addiction is to address the issues and circumstances that led to addiction in the first place. Self-analysis can be a great thing and work for a lot of people. Some may need guidance in this area to help identify the root cause. A professional, a mentor or a friend or family member can provide the assistance. Once the

---

[1] Dr. Gabor Maté. "How Trauma Leads To Addiction." *YouTube*, uploaded by Better Chapter, April 4, 2022,
https://www.youtube.com/watch?v=TUTqOr0w8Hc.

source of the trauma is recognized, the person can begin the healing process.

# CHAPTER FOUR

## THE ESCAPISM TRAP

Escapism can be defined as the tendency to seek distraction and relief from unpleasant realities, especially by seeking entertainment or engaging in fantasy. When faced with unpleasant realities such as poverty, grief, depression, anxiety, stress, health issues, family issues, relationship issues, and uncertainty of the future, some people fall victim to drug addiction while using drugs to try and escape the unpleasant reality they are facing. Escapism can become a coping mechanism for some people, especially those with unresolved trauma in their past. They think that if they ignore their problems, they will not have to deal with them. However, engaging in escapism usually compounds their problems later down the line. Instead of engaging in escapism, individuals should be encouraged to deal with the root cause of these unpleasant circumstances head on and conquer them once and for all.

Drug and/or alcohol abuse are not the only way to fall into the escapism trap. I don't drink alcohol and I have never used drugs, but I once fell into the escapism trap myself.

I do not have an addictive personality, but after my father passed away in 2018, I fell into depression and was overwhelmed by my newfound responsibilities. I wasn't as mentally prepared for these responsibilities as I thought I would be. As a result, I buried myself in an online video game. At the time, I recognized that I was using it as a form of escapism. However, I didn't realize the dangers of that escapism. It would come back to haunt me.

I played that game every day for hours on end, spending way too much money on it and ignoring all my responsibilities, especially paying my bills. A few times when Ashley would see me playing the game, she would bust my chops and say, "Looks like you have a little addiction going there." I would joke back, "Yeah, I have a $150/week habit."

While it took me three months to recognize I had gotten addicted to the game, it took another nine months before I was able to break that addiction, despite the fact that I was tired of investing time and money into the game. In addition to my father's death and newfound responsibilities for which I originally got addicted, I used the game as escapism once again when a close friend passed away six months after my father.

Finally, after much conviction from the Holy Spirit for slacking off on writing this book because I was spending so much time on that game, one evening, I decided to abstain from the game for one day to work on this book. I never picked up that game again. I was miraculously delivered! Now, I admit that I have been tempted to play the game when I'm really bored. However, I have recognized, through my experience dealing with friends who have battled drug addiction, that not only can I not do that, but I cannot even entertain the thought.

The consequences of my escapism included falling behind on most of my bills. My water was shut off briefly as a result. My house almost went into Tax Sale, which created a huge financial strain (I had to come up with $3,800 within two months), which in turn made me further behind on my other bills. Also, I was not able to afford to fix my vehicle. Two years after it broke down, it still had not been repaired as a result. I eventually had to junk the vehicle because it was unfixable after sitting idle for so long. It took another year before I was able to buy another car, which caused my travel expenses to skyrocket when I was forced to take an Uber or Lyft back and forth to work every day.

While I was fortunate enough not to have resorted to something as destructive as drugs to escape my unpleasant realities, I have known people who did. Needless to say, drugs did nothing to help them overcome their unpleasant realities. Often, it compounded them.

My cousin got addicted to opiate pain medication because of injuries sustained in a car accident several years ago. She had multiple prescriptions and they would often cause her to be knocked out for half the day. Naturally, she was unable to care for her children properly. Years later, she decided to stop taking the opiate pain medication because she couldn't function. However, she replaced the medication with marijuana. While she said it helped with the pain, she did admit one time she smoked it to escape her problems. She just wanted to numb herself to her lousy life. She didn't want to deal with life's struggles and ignored her responsibilities. It came to a point where her children, who were grown by then, treated her like she was the child and they were the adults. Her lack of responsibility almost got them evicted from their apartment on several occasions as well.

My cousin's circumstance is a clear example of how using drugs to escape from reality will only cause more problems thereby worsening whatever situation they may be faced with.

# CHAPTER FIVE

## COVERING EMOTIONAL SCARS

In order to cover emotional scars, some people resort to using drugs. These emotional scars can include grief, depression, anxiety, bullying, and psychological trauma, typically as a result of being the victim of a crime. I know people who were victims of both violent and sex related crimes. These individuals often turned to drugs to mask the emotional scars of those incidents. Not only were some of these people not addicts, but they had never even tried drugs before. They were desperate to find something to avoid dealing with their emotional scars and unfortunately, turned to drugs to do so.

I also had friends who turned to drugs to conceal the emotional pain from the unexpected death of a close family member. The pain of the loss was so great they couldn't handle the trauma. They were so overcome with grief that they chose to numb themselves to the psychological pain by using drugs.

Even if people don't resort to drugs to deal with their emotional scars, some opt to seek some sort of therapy to deal with the trauma. This method of coping can be hit or miss depending on the individual. While seeking professional help to deal with emotional scars is much better than just numbing pain with drugs, it is not the ideal or permanent solution to this issue, which we will discuss later.

Former NFL wide receiver Percy Harvin acknowledged he combated anxiety during his playing days by self-medicating with marijuana, saying that he played every game of his career while high. "There's not a game—there's not a game I played that I wasn't high," Harvin told Bleacher Report in a video interview published on October 2019.[2] The purpose of Harvin's disclosure, in his opinion, was to make the world see that, "…it's not a stigma and people doing it and getting into a whole bunch of trouble. It's just people that's just living regular life that just got deficiencies or maybe just want to enjoy themselves. It's a natural way to do so."

Here again, we see the marijuana user trying to justify their drug use. Most marijuana users I have encountered, especially millennials, often engage in this type of behavior. Marijuana use is often justified by them for medicinal reasons to treat anxiety and depression, which often stem from emotional scars that are the result of emotional trauma, such as abuse. While some marijuana users claim it provides a beneficial effect in dealing with their past emotional trauma, it doesn't cure them. It just covers up their pain so they can function better. I have often used the Nyquil analogy in explaining this.

When a person is suffering from a bad cold, often times, they will take Nyquil, which doesn't cure them of their cold. It only suppresses the symptoms so they can function better. Anxiety and depression are symptoms of a deeper-rooted problem. Marijuana doesn't deliver its users from their emotional scars and the resulting effects. In fact, it can cause additional negative effects in a person's life. Marijuana also doesn't allow them to completely heal from their past emotional trauma. In subsequent chapters, we will see the true cure for these ails.

---

[2] Shanna McCarriston, "Percy Harvin smoked weed before every NFL game he played to combat his anxiety," *CBS Sports*, (October 2, 2019), accessed November 2, 2024, at: https://www.cbssports.com/nfl/news/percy-harvin-smoked-weed-before-every-nfl-game-he-played-to-combat-his-anxiety/.

# CHAPTER SIX

# PEER PRESSURE AND MARIJUANA

Peer pressure is defined as "influence from members of one's peer group." Examples of negative peer pressure can include trying to talk someone into trying drugs, cigarettes, alcohol, and sex. Teens are especially vulnerable to peer pressure. During a teen's formative years, peer pressure is at its greatest in one's life. The problem has been compounded even further in the age of social media. Some cannot handle the pressure to be themselves and go their own way and wind up succumbing to peer pressure. Some of the reasons for succumbing to peer pressure include a desire to fit in, to avoid rejection and gain social acceptance, hormonal inconsistencies, personal/social confusion and/or anxiety, and a lack of structure at home. All too often, teens are peer pressured into using drugs, with marijuana being the most common.

Amongst millennials, the attitude towards this drug is much more lax than compared to older generations. It is socially acceptable to them and deemed harmless by them as well. Some claim that smoking marijuana has medicinal and psychological benefits. Some even refute its addictive qualities. To a teen, smoking marijuana can be a means to numb the pain, struggle and torment of their unique teen issues.

While some marijuana users refute that it is addictive, this is simply not true. Delta-9-tetrahydrocannabinol, or THC, is the addictive main active chemical in marijuana. When smoked, THC quickly passes through the lungs and into the bloodstream, thus carrying it to various organs, including the brain, where the bulk of cannabinoid receptors reside. These receptors mediate the high via a variety of complex mechanisms.

Marijuana use can have both short-term and long-term effects on a person. The short-term effects are:

- Short-term memory problems
- Severe anxiety, including fear that one is being watched or followed (paranoia)
- Very strange behavior such as seeing, hearing or smelling things that aren't there and/or not being able to tell imagination from reality (psychosis)
- Panic
- Hallucinations
- Loss of sense of personal identity
- Lowered reaction time
- Increased heart rate (risk of heart attack)
- Increased risk of stroke
- Problems with coordination (impairing safe driving or playing sports)
- Sexual problems (for males)
- Up to seven times more likely to contract sexually transmitted infections than non-users (for females)

The long-term effects are:

- Decline in IQ (up to eight points if prolonged use started in adolescent age)
- Poor school performance and higher chance of dropping out
- Impaired thinking and ability to learn and perform complex tasks
- Lower life satisfaction

- Addiction (about 9% of adults and 17% of people who started smoking as teens)
- Potential development of opiate abuse
- Relationship problems and/or intimate partner violence
- Antisocial behavior including stealing money or lying
- Financial difficulties
- Increased welfare dependence
- Greater chances of being unemployed or not getting good jobs

In addition, according to the State of California Proposition 65 warning list,[3] exposure to cannabis smoke can cause developmental harm and cancer. More specifically, it warns:

- Smoking or being heavily exposed to cannabis smoke during pregnancy can harm the development of the child. It may affect the child's birthweight, behavior and learning ability.
- Smoking or being heavily exposed to cannabis smoke may increase the risk of cancer.

They additionally warn that cannabis smoke contains several thousand different chemicals, some of which are on the Proposition 65 warning list. These include:

- Chemicals that can affect the baby when the mother is exposed to them during pregnancy such as THC, which may affect behavior, learning ability and susceptibility to drug addiction in offspring.

---

[3] *Proposition 65 Warnings Website*, "Cannabis (Marijuana) Smoke," accessed October 28, 2024, at: https://www.p65warnings.ca.gov/fact-sheets/cannabis-marijuana-smoke.

- Other chemicals that cause cancer and/or reproductive harm such as benzene, benzo[a]pyrene, 1.3-butadiene, cadmium, carbon monoxide, hexavalent chromium, formaldehyde, lead, and nickel.

A 2024 study led by Dr. Niels Kokot, professor of clinical otolaryngology-head and neck surgery at the Keck School of Southern California in Los Angeles, shows that marijuana smokers who partake in heavy marijuana use are "significantly more likely to develop head and neck cancers compared to those who do not use cannabis."[4] Head and neck cancers include cancers of the throat, trachea, salivary glands, as well as the mouth. The study focused on people diagnosed with a problematic cannabis-related disorder. Kokot's research team wrote, "We found that the relative risk of developing head and neck cancer for those with cannabis-related disorders ranged from 3.5 to 5 times that of those without cannabis-related disorders." The study mainly focuses on cannabis usage by way of smoking "as it is most commonly consumed by smoking," Kokot wrote. "The association we found likely pertains mainly to smoked cannabis."

Dr. Michael Blasco, the director of the head and neck oncology and reconstruction at Northwell Health in Staten Island, NY weighed in on Dr. Kokot's research. "Now we know that there is a link between cannabis use and head and neck cancer – I would say that we've proven the link," Blasco stated. "We don't necessarily know what the threshold is that seems to greatly increase the risk, but we know that heavy users have higher rates, so I would 100 percent tell patients

---

[4] Blake Wolf, "New Study Claims Certain Cancers Could Be Linked To 'Heavy Cannabis Use,'" *One America News*, (August 8, 2024), accessed November 2, 2024, at https://www.oann.com/newsroom/new-study-claims-certain-cancers-could-be-linked-to-heavy-cannabis-use/.

there's a link between head and neck cancer and cannabis use."

Blasco went on to say, "This is part of a growing body of literature that's showing that there are measurable negative health effects from cannabis use. Whether that's effects on the lungs, whether that's effects on the mood and addiction. And then this is part of a growing body of literature that suggests association with cancers. So, we're learning more and more about the long-term health effects of cannabis."

## My Observation of Marijuana Users

I have known two individuals whom I would consider to have been addicted to marijuana. The first is a 19-year-old male. He used to smoke marijuana every weekend while staying overnight at a hotel during the rehearsal weekends of our drum and bugle corps. This guy never seemed to have money for food, as I bought him lunch nearly every weekend, but he always seemed to have money for the marijuana he smoked. He chose marijuana over food. If that isn't an addiction, I don't know what is. What was even more frustrating was that he stood to inherit $50,000 from his grandfather, with the only stipulation being that he had to prove he could be responsible. He just could not do it. He couldn't even hold a job for more than two weeks. Fortunately, he later turned around his life and now owns a successful business.

The second individual is a 21-year-old female. She originally started smoking marijuana in her teens because of the "cool factor" but given her family's history of addiction, she soon became addicted. Despite my warnings to her about her family's history of addiction and the fact that she hated being around her aunts when they were high, she failed to heed my warnings. She quit sports in high school, which she was good at, because they started drug testing the student athletes. She has not been able to hold a job for more than a week, on the rare occasions she was actually seeking employment. When she does seek employment, her options are limited because she only applies to companies that do not do drug tests. Apparently, smoking marijuana is more important to her than getting a job and making money so she can eat. She currently has no ambitions for the future and no drive to do anything with her life. The drug is totally holding her back. She was a smart and talented individual who had a lot of potential and plans for the future until she got addicted to marijuana. How sad!

## The Ricky Williams Story

Probably the saddest story concerning marijuana addiction is the story of former NFL star running back Ricky Williams. He was drafted fifth overall in the 1999 NFL Draft by the New Orleans Saints. He played with the Saints for three seasons before being traded to the Miami Dolphins in 2002. It was announced on May 14, 2004 that Williams tested positive for marijuana in December 2003 and faced a $650,000 fine and a four-game suspension for violating the NFL's substance-abuse policy. He previously tested positive for marijuana shortly after he joined the Dolphins. Before training camp was to begin in July 2004, Williams publicly disclosed his intent to retire from professional football.

Rumored to have failed a third drug test before announcing his retirement, Williams made his retirement official on August 2, 2004. He was ineligible to play for the 2004 season, and studied Ayurveda, the ancient Indian system of holistic medicine, at the California College of Ayurveda that autumn in Grass Valley, California. The Dolphins finished the 2004 season with a 4–12 record.

Williams maintains that he does not regret the retirement decision. He thinks that it was the "most positive thing" he has ever done in his life, allowing him time to find himself.

On February 20, 2006, the NFL announced that Williams had violated the NFL drug policy for the fourth time. His mother reportedly said she did not think it was another marijuana violation and that he may have been in India when he was supposed to be tested. On April 25, 2006, Williams was suspended for the entire 2006 season. It has been suggested that the substance may have been an herb related to his interest in holistic medicine.

On May 11, 2007, an anonymous source reported that Williams had failed a drug test again. The source indicated that NFL medical advisors had recommended to the commissioner that Williams not be allowed to apply for reinstatement that September. Williams adhered to a strict regimen of multiple drug tests per week in 2007 as part of his attempt to be reinstated by the NFL. He practiced yoga, which, he claimed, helped him to stop using marijuana.

As you can see from Ricky Williams' story, his addiction to marijuana caused him to fail to honor his contract with his team, leaving them in a lurch right before training camp, which in turn led his team to finish with a poor record that year. He gave up millions of dollars in income as a result of fines, suspensions and early retirement because he did not want to stop smoking marijuana. Smoking marijuana was that important to him. It took precedence over everything in his life at the time. It was more important to him than his contract, his team, his teammates, and his income. In addition, his reputation took a huge hit in the process. Fortunately, Willimas seems to have turned his life around and put marijuana aside.

## Marijuana Legalization

Since the early 2000s, more and more States, Democratic controlled ones in particular, have attempted to legalize marijuana. The most common argument in favor of the legalization is the tax revenue it would generate. In fact, this is the only reason want to legalize it. They seem to be indifferent to the negative consequences of marijuana usage as long as the tax revenue keeps coming in.

Some also argue that legalization would help alleviate the prison overpopulation as most inmates are incarcerated for drug offenses. However, these arguments ignore the fact that marijuana is an illegal substance according to federal law.

In addition, they disregard that marijuana, like any other drug, can be addictive. Many States, including my home State of New Jersey, currently do not have enough space available in drug rehabilitation facilities for the number of addicts who need it or are required by law to enter one. I have personally witnessed people having to wait up to two months for an opening. For those on Methadone, the wait can be up to six months as not all drug rehabilitation facilities take Methadone patients. This waiting time doesn't change if admission is required by a court order. Often, the courts must be provided with proof of the long waiting time. Of course, the number one danger is that the drug addict could easily overdose while they are waiting to enter a drug rehabilitation facility. In my opinion, legalizing marijuana would create a new generation of drug addicts. It will also extend the waiting time for all drug addicts who need or are required to enter a drug rehabilitation facility.

Some States have already legalized medical marijuana and are attempting to legalize its recreational use. However, this transition has caused numerous issues in the supply chain with both medical marijuana patients and their dispensaries.

Both are concerned that those who need marijuana for medical issues may not be able to receive it due to the increased demand caused by a large influx of recreational users.

Some advocates of recreational marijuana usage have even fought for the right to be able to smoke up to one minute before they clock into work, saying it is on their time. I hate to inform these misguided individuals but if a person is high one minute before they punch into work, they are still high after they punch into work. This would create a huge liability issue for employers. If I were a business owner, there is no way I would let one of these individuals operate any machinery or any piece of equipment in my company. The risk of injury and damage would be too great. The quality of the employees' work would suffer as well.

Additionally, there is the issue of all the demonic doorways that will be opened in the lives of marijuana users. In a later chapter, we will learn about how marijuana is a "gateway drug."

# CHAPTER SEVEN

## PHYSICAL PAIN KILLERS

Individuals often use drugs to kill physical pain. While most don't opt for hardcore opiates, such as heroin, right away, they often become addicted to opiate pain medication that was prescribed by a doctor for a legitimate reason. When the opiate pain medication runs out and they can longer get the medication from their doctor, they will either go "doctor shopping" until they find one who will prescribe the medication they need, buy the medication off the street, or turn to illegal opiates like heroin.

Ashley is an example of the latter. Her doctor prescribed her opiate pain medication after she suffered injuries in a car accident. After a while, she got hooked on the medication. When she could no longer get the medication legally, someone "recommended" she try heroin, thus starting her long struggle with drug addiction.

I know another person who had been on Methadone for years and when they finally stopped taking it, they didn't realize how much physical pain it had covered-up. Within a couple of months, she turned to heroin to cope with the pain because she refused to be a slave to Methadone again. Two months later, she overdosed and died.

I have another friend who was prescribed Percocet by her doctor for pain due to a back injury from an auto accident. One day, she was told by her doctor that her urine came back "dirty" and her prescription was cut off. Once her withdrawal symptoms started, she asked a friend, who she knew was a heroin addict, if she was able to acquire Percocet for her off the street, which she was able to do for a while. However, her friend's sources eventually dried up. She then tried to convince my friend that heroin was just as effective as a pain killer as Percocet was, lasted longer and was much cheaper. She kept on pressuring her and putting that thought into her head over and over again until my friend finally broke down and tried heroin. It didn't take long for her to get addicted and she has regretted that decision ever since.

## The Opioid Epidemic in America

The opioid epidemic in America was a result of doctors overprescribing opiate pain medication. Often, these doctors' first go to was to prescribe their patients a pill. As has been revealed since then, big pharmaceutical companies ("Big Pharma") have been paying doctors to push their pills for many years and recently have lost class action lawsuits as a result.

To help combat this problem, in 2010, President Barack Obama signed into law the Physician Payments Sunshine Act, which required disclosure of any payment over $10 to medical professionals from pharmaceutical, insurance or other providers seeking reimbursement under Medicare, Medicaid and Children's Health Insurance Program (CHIP).

When President Donald J. Trump took office in January 2017, the opioid crisis was devastating communities across America. Opioid overdoses accounted for more than 42,000 of these deaths, more than any previous year on record. Nearly 64,000 Americans died from a drug overdose. Because of this, President Trump committed to fighting the opioid epidemic in America. In October 2017, he declared the opioid crisis a public health emergency. The Trump Administration applied an all-of-government approach to the epidemic, taking an extraordinary range of actions that reflected the President's commitment to stopping the crisis. President Trump's Initiative to Stop Opioid Abuse, unveiled in 2018, confronted the driving forces behind the opioid crisis. Part 1 reduced demand and over-prescription, including educating Americans about the dangers of opioid misuse. Part 2 cut down on the supply of illicit drugs by cracking down on the international and domestic drug supply chains that devastated American communities. Part 3 helped those struggling with addiction through evidence-based treatment and recovery support services.

Among the historic actions taken:

- As of October 2018, the Trump Administration had secured $6 billion in new funding over a two-year window to fight opioid abuse.
- To curb over-prescription, the President implemented a Safer Prescribing Plan that would cut opioid prescription fills by one-third within three years.
- President Trump fought to keep dangerous drugs out of the United States by securing land borders, ports of entry and waterways against smuggling.
- In 2018, President Trump worked with Congress to pass the SUPPORT Act, the single largest legislative package addressing a single drug crisis in history. Unfortunately, although the SUPPORT Act had bipartisan support, it expired on September 30, 2023 before the U.S. House of Representatives was able to vote for its reauthorization. Drug abuse advocates believe that action will be taken and it will be passed in the near future.

The Trump Administration's actions have resulted in the following:

- The number of first-time heroin users ages 12 and older fell by more than 50 percent in July 2017. Between President Trump's Inauguration and October 2018, high-dose opioid prescriptions fell by 16 percent.
- In July 2017, the Department of Justice shutdown the country's biggest Darknet distributor of drugs. That same fiscal year, U.S. Immigration and Customs Enforcement took more than 2,300 pounds of fentanyl off the streets.
- In terms of helping those struggling with addiction, there was a 20 percent increase in young adults receiving outpatient treatment. And in 2017, America had an increase in the number of patients ages 12 and older with illicit drug-use disorders being treated at specialty facilities and private provider offices.

## Fentanyl Crisis and the Southern Border

As a result of the Biden Administration's open border policy, drug trafficking through the southern border of the United States has increased exponentially since 2021. Mexican drug cartels often use innocent women and children as drug mules to smuggle them into the country. One of the primary drugs of choice to smuggle is fentanyl.

Fentanyl is an illegal opiate drug that is one hundred times more potent than heroin. Most fentanyl coming through the southern border is manufactured in China. It makes one wonder if the Chinese fentanyl trade is China's revenge for its losses in the First and Second Opium Wars of the late 1800's.

Because fentanyl is so much more potent than heroin, it has greatly increased the death rate from overdoses. According to an article published on KFF.org, "Fentanyl-involved opioid deaths surged more than 23-fold over the last decade, while prescription opioid deaths remained steady and heroin deaths declined. Fentanyl deaths more than doubled during the pandemic, increasing from 36,359 in 2019 to 73,838 in 2022."[5] For those who would like to learn more about this subject, read the Drug Enforcement Administration's "National Drug Threat Assessment 2024" report.[6]

While the statistics regarding fentanyl deaths are widely reported in the media, I was curious about what was causing the death increase amongst fentanyl users. Was it because opiate addicts were using the same amount of fentanyl as they did heroin? According to a friend of mine who is a former heroin and fentanyl user, it is more complicated than just the increased potency of fentanyl verses heroin. She said it is almost impossible to find pure heroin (which would explain the decrease in heroin related deaths in the last few years). Mostly, fentanyl is on the streets now. She further explained that drug dealers mix fentanyl with heroin and baby aspirin. This mixture is then divided up into sellable portions. However, the admixture of the three substances can vary from portion to portion. A user may get a batch that is 80% baby aspirin. Another time, they may get a batch that is 80% heroin. If they are extremely unlucky, they may receive a batch that is 90% fentanyl. Because the mixtures with high amounts of baby aspirin or heroin are not as potent as others that contain large amounts of fentanyl, addicts think they can

---

[5] Heather Saunders, Nirmita Panchal, and Sasha Zitter, "Opioid Deaths Fell in Mid-2023, But Progress Is Uneven and Future Trends are Uncertain," *KFF*, (September 23, 2024), accessed November 30, 2024, at: https://www.kff.org/mental-health/issue-brief/opioid-deaths-fell-in-mid-2023-but-progress-is-uneven-and-future-trends-are-uncertain/#:~:text=Fentanyl%2Dinvolved%20opioid%20deaths%20surged,in%202022%20(Figure%201).

[6] *U.S. Department of Justice Drug Enforcement Administration*, "National Drug Threatt Assessment 2024," accessed November 30, 2024, at: https://www.dea.gov/sites/default/files/2024-05/NDTA_2024.pdf.

handle more and subsequently take more. The fentanyl deaths come into play when they get an unlucky batch with high fentanyl content. My friend said addicts really are playing Russian roulette with their life every time they take that stuff. She is very grateful that she never experienced an overdose of any kind and believes God was watching over her for a greater purpose.

## Pill Pushers and Pharmacies Sued

In mid-2020, Swiss drug maker Norvartis agreed to pay more than $729 million to settle a lawsuit filed in relation to an alleged kickback scheme. The whistleblower suit was filed against Norvantis in 2011. The company was accused of paying kickbacks to doctors in order to prescribe its drugs, including speaking fees for supposed educational events.

In February 2023, four pharmaceutical companies— Johnson & Johnson, AmerisourceBergen, Cardinal Health, and McKesson—agreed to pay $26 billion in class-action lawsuit settlements for their part in the opioid crisis.

CVS, Walgreens and Walmart have all been sued in class-action lawsuits for filling fraudulent prescriptions of opiate pain medication. In December 2022, CVS and Walgreens agreed to pay more than $10 billion to several States in lawsuit settlements brought against them alleging their roles in the opioid crisis. CVS would pay nearly $5 billion over 10 years, while Walgreens would pay $5.7 billion over 15 years, according to statements released by State Attorney Generals.

On December 20, 2022, Walmart announced it surpassed the first threshold required for finalizing the company's $3.1 billion nationwide opioid settlement framework announced on November 15, 2022. The company has settlement agreements with all 50 States, including four States that previously settled with the company, as well as the District of

Columbia, Puerto Rico, and three other U.S. territories, that are intended to resolve substantially all opioids-related lawsuits brought by State and local governments against Walmart. The participation exceeded the 43 States that were required to join the nationwide settlement framework by December 15, 2022 for it to move forward. The settlement is currently being paid out.[7]

[7] *National Opioid Settlements*, "National Opioid Settlements Dashboard - CVS, Walgreens, and Walmart," accessed November 30, 2024, at: https://nationalopioidsettlement.com/wp-content/uploads/2024/11/CVS-Walgreens-Walmart-Payment-Dashboard-11.13.24.pdf.

# CHAPTER EIGHT

# THE DANGERS OF DRUGS ADDICTION

The dangers of drug addiction are numerous. These dangers include the use of poor judgement, health issues, financial issues, social issues, mortality issues, mental health issues, legal issues, paternity issues, and moral issues. Let's examine the effect each issue can have on a drug addict's life.

## Poor Judgement

Drugs tend to contribute to individuals using poor judgement in general. This poor judgement can often lead to one or more of the above mentioned issues.

The Bible teaches us to be sober minded:

*"Therefore, with minds that are alert and fully sober, set your hope on the grace to be brought to you when Jesus Christ is revealed at his coming"* (1 Peter 1:13 NIV).

*"Be alert and of sober mind. Your enemy the devil prowls around like a roaring lion looking for someone to devour"* (1 Peter 5:8 NIV).

The Bible also warns us of the dangers of using addictive substances such as alcohol and drugs:

*"Wine is a mocker and beer a brawler; whoever is led astray by them is not wise"* (Proverbs 20:1 NIV).

*"It is not for kings, Lemuel—it is not for kings to drink wine, not for rulers to crave beer, lest they drink and forget what has been decreed, and deprive all the oppressed of their rights"* (Proverbs 31:4-5 NIV).

*"Do not get drunk on wine, which leads to debauchery. Instead, be filled with the Spirit,"* (Ephesians 5:18 NIV).

While the above Scriptures specifically talk about alcohol, the same principal applies to drugs because they have the same effect on a person who uses them. It causes poor judgement, which often leads to other negative behavior.

I knew someone who was going to a Methadone clinic to try and control their opiate addiction. One day, she arrived too late. Not wanting to feel the agonizing withdrawal effects of not receiving her daily dose of Methadone, she saw someone across the street from the clinic who was selling drugs. She said to herself, "Fuck it," and proceeded to purchase some heroin to make up for her missed dose of Methadone. Her first mistake was saying what she said. That statement violates my "Golden Rule of Making Decisions," which appears in my book, *Golden Rules: Rules for Making Wise Choices*. This golden rule states:

*"Whenever you say to yourself, 'Fuck it,' you're about to make a huge mistake."*

Employees of the Methadone clinic saw the woman purchasing the drugs and she was booted from the program. She wound up having to travel thirty minutes away to another Methadone clinic, which was located in a bad neighborhood, to get her daily dose. Most of the time, she was forced to take the bus so it wound up being a three hour round trip. Talk about a daily inconvenience! It took over a year to get reinstated to the clinic she got kicked out of, which was located closer to where she lived. That one bad decision affected her for a long time and could have potentially caused other negative issues in her life.

## Health Issues

Drug addiction can have an adverse effect on a person's physical health. In the height of Ashley's addiction, she nearly destroyed the veins in her arms from shooting up. She actually dug a hole in her arm with a needle once because she was desperate to find a vein. That incident required medical attention as the hole got infected. When she could no longer find a vein in her arm, she would use veins in her hands, feet and breasts. Even the Methadone she was on at the time to help curb her drug cravings caused adverse medical conditions, including high blood pressure.

Some other health issues that can result from drug use include dental issues, organ failure, heart failure, and brain damage. I have seen all these medical conditions in the lives of my friends who were addicts. I have witnessed first-hand the trials and heartaches that those health issues can cause for both the addict and the ones who love them. After my friend passed away from a drug overdose, she was tested to see if her organs could be donated, as she had elected to be an organ donor. None of her organs were viable for donation because of her lifestyle. This led me to believe that if she had not died of a drug overdose, she would have passed away in a few years due to some other health related issue.

In addition, the likelihood of contracting a sexually transmitted disease (STD) is greatly increased. Women who engage in sexual acts to pay for their drug habit or people who have sex with a partner who may have already contracted an STD are more susceptible than most. These women tend to have a high number of sexual partners, some of which may be total strangers, which greatly increases their odds of contracting an STD. Intervenes (IV) drug users are also more likely to contract diseases such as Hepatitis C and HIV/AIDS, especially if they share needles with others.

## Financial Issues

Drug addiction can cause financial hardship because the user needs more and more money to feed their habit. They will steal from their jobs, friends and loved ones. The addict doesn't care if the money has been earmarked for something important either. All they are thinking about is their next fix. Some examples of this behavior include an instance when Ashley once stole $500 from her father that her sister had given to him for their mother's tombstone. Needless to say, both her sister and their father were livid with Ashley. Another time, Ashley's brother-in-law found some of his tools that had been stolen in a local pawn shop a few weeks after they went missing. Ashley and her addict sisters would often break into each other's bedrooms to steal money, prescription medication and cigarettes. This caused a lot of anger, tension and mistrust between them. Their father had to hide and lock his wallet and cigarettes in his car so they wouldn't be stolen by his daughters while he slept. That is no way to live!

## Social Issues

Social issues related to drug addiction include the stereotypical, and all too common, shunning of the drug addicted individual that we examined in Chapter One. This is amplified if the addict has been caught stealing from friends and loved ones to pay for their addiction. Coupled with this is a lack of trust toward the addict. This is a big one because, as I've often said, "Where there is no trust, there is no relationship." I know people who have shunned their family members who were addicted to drugs because of the adverse behavior the addicts displayed toward them. I also know one individual who would often be unfairly lumped in with her three drug addicted siblings. People would automatically assume because all her siblings were drug addicts, she must be one too, even though she didn't use drugs.

Often, shunning leads the addict to only hang out with other addicts or people who are willing to take advantage of the addict, usually offering to exchange money for sex. Addicts who are hard up to support their habits will engage in this behavior as they see it as easy money. To the addict, it is a much faster and easier way of making large sums of money than working a legitimate job, which they struggle to hold anyway.

When Ashley went to a drug rehabilitation facility early in our friendship, they made visitors go through a mandatory one-hour family therapy session before they were allowed to visit their loved one. The biggest takeaway I got from those sessions was how important it is for addicts to stay away from people, places and things that are triggers for their addiction. This is something Ashley struggled with for nearly four years, since most of the people she knew, including other family members, were triggers. She struggled mightily to summon the will to cut people out of her life, especially family members. Thank God that after she gave her life to Jesus, she was finally able to get a revelation of the importance of this and God gave her the strength and will to do so.

Who an individual hangs around is extremely relevant. I have learned from my own personal experience that people tend to act like those they spend time with. Years later, I heard Terri Savelle Foy confirm this when she said, "You are the sum of the five people you hang out with the most." Early in my Christian walk, I struggled with this. At times, I was hanging out with my new Christian friends and at other times I was hanging out with my old non-Christian friends. I tended to act like whoever I was hanging out with. I had one foot in the Kingdom of God and one foot in the world so my "walk" was funny. I wasn't able to get my "walk" straightened out for years until I was able to cut my non-Christian friends out of my life. While my struggle dealt with my Christian walk, anyone can see the principle in action from my experience. This parallels the addicts' need to cut certain people out of their lives who are negative influences on them.

## Mortality Issues

Mortality issues usually involve being the victim of a crime in relation to the addicts' addiction. A common crime involves a drug deal that has gone wrong for whatever reason. Two incidents like this occurred in Ashley's family.

One of her sisters was shot twice in a robbery attempt as her and a male friend were in a bad neighborhood asking where they could buy Xanax. Naturally, the criminals knew that since they were there seeking to buy drugs, they must have a lot of money on them. Hence, they were robbed and she was shot once in the left hip and once in her right femur, shattering it. She spent a month in the hospital and another two months in a physical rehabilitation facility recovering from her injuries. Two years later, she still walks awkwardly with a cane and may require a hip replacement. She is in constant pain and is legally disabled for an indefinite period of time. Being a single mom of an autistic son, the result of her ordeal makes it even harder for her to take care of her son. She is blessed to be alive today because if the gunman had aimed higher, she probably wouldn't be.

Another incident involved one of Ashley's cousins. Her and her fiancée were planning to travel to Florida and before they left on their trip, decided to buy a whole bunch of drugs. When the dealers saw all that money (around $3,000), they robbed them. The fiancée, whom the drug dealers didn't like, was shot six times in the chest and killed. Ashley's cousin was shot in the head twice and left for dead simply because she had witnessed the shooting. Fortunately, by the grace of God, she survived and was able to lead the police to capture the culprits. However, she still has bullet fragments in her brain and is permanently disabled. She has no motor control of her legs below her knees, due to the brain damage caused by the bullet, and can only walk using leg braces and a cane.

A friend of mine has a boyfriend who hangs out with drug dealers and, for some dumb reason, they give him credit for the drugs he uses. Talk about bad business practices! Drug addicts are some of the most untrustworthy people we will ever meet. Expecting them to actually pay their debts is a big leap of faith on the dealers' part. With this particular individual, he would lie to them about when he would pay and avoid them at all costs when he didn't have the means to pay them back. This was because he barely worked and just mooched off of his disabled girlfriend. As a result, he had a gun pointed at him multiple times and his girlfriend's family was threatened with being shot on several occasions as well. Because of his poor decisions, not only was his girlfriend's family put in mortal danger several times, but his girlfriend also had to bail him out and pay his debts to his drug dealers just to avoid any harm coming to her family. This in turn caused repeated financial strain for herself as well as causing a lot of stress and tension in their relationship and in their household.

All too often, the primary mortality issue addicts must face is a possible drug overdose. As the addict builds up a tolerance to their drug of choice over time, they need more and more of the drug in order to get the same effect. It can get so bad that it can lead to an overdose. This can cause hospitalization and/or death. I have witnessed both. It is especially traumatic when a close friend or family member overdoses. Thank God, the overall statistical numbers of overdoses started to decline during the Trump Administration due to increased attention and emphasis on the Opioid Epidemic, greater law enforcement and interdiction at the southern border of the United States. Unfortunately, this trend was reversed in recent years due to the fentanyl crisis which was a result of the Biden Administration's open borders policy.

Another factor, which aided in the decrease of overdose deaths, was the fact that more and more First Responders started carrying Naloxone in the late 2010's. Naloxone is more commonly referred to by the brand name NARCAN. It is a medication that is used for the treatment of an opioid emergency or a possible opioid overdose with signs of breathing problems and severe sleepiness or not being able to respond. Naloxone blocks the effects of opioids, especially decreased breathing. In March 2023, the U.S. Food and Drug Administration approved NARCAN for over-the-counter use. It is believed that having NARCAN more easily available and at the ready will help decrease opioid related overdoses. According to a predictive model of the Stanford Lancet Commission on the North American Opioid Crises, expanding naloxone availability by 30% would prevent approximately 144,000 deaths over five years and 301,900 deaths over ten years.[8]

More recently, someone I know accidently overdosed on Fentanyl and nearly died. Thankfully, NARCAN was kept in

---

[8] *National Library of Medicine,* "The FDA approves the second OTC naloxone – a step toward opioid crisis mitigation," accessed December 8, 2024, at: https://pmc.ncbi.nlm.nih.gov/articles/PMC10720828/#:~:text=The%20first %20OTC%20naloxone%20spray,in%20July%20this%20year1.

the house for just such an emergency. It took two shots of the medication to revive her. Thankfully, she did not have any adverse health effects, other than the black eye her roommate gave her trying to wake her up. Thank God she survived this accidental overdose and this incident was the wakeup call she needed. She was scared when she realized that she nearly killed herself. She swore to me the next day that she was done with drugs. However, this turned out to not be the case. She overdosed again, but I was there and able to get an ambulance to arrive in time to give her NARCAN. Unfortunately, she died from another overdose a few weeks later after the members of her household had moved out and she was basically left alone. Her landlord's girlfriend woke up for work one morning and found her dead on the bathroom floor.

## Mental Health Issues

Mental health issues can range from depression and suicidal tendencies to temporary or permanent psychosis and possibly even brain damage. Twice, Ashley had to be admitted to a psychiatric hospital. The first time, she was admitted by an emergency room doctor because she was having suicidal thoughts. The second time, her sister and I were forced to call Adult Protective Services (APS) to take Ashley into protective custody. She was clearly not in her right mind. After four days, I began to think she had done permanent brain damage to herself. She was in that facility a day longer than they were supposed to keep her and the facility planned to send her to a long-term psychiatric facility the next afternoon. Thankfully, she snapped out of it by the next day and she did not sustain any brain damage.

One of Ashley's family members was in a long-term psychiatric facility for years as a result of his drug addiction.

He was diagnosed with "multiple personality disorder" and also suffered from bipolar disorder.

Mental health issues can affect those left behind after their loved one died of a drug overdose. A friend of mine still hasn't gotten over the death of her mother and the sister she was closest to, even though it has been years since their passing. Her sister's children have suffered mental trauma as a result of their mother's death. They felt like their mother abandoned them for their infant brother who had tragically passed away a year prior.

## Legal Issues

Legal issues usually involve some sort of incarceration and/or probation. Ashley got arrested in an incident that took place right before we started hanging out together. One night, she was getting a ride from another woman, who was also a drug addict. They got pulled over by the police after the other woman ran a stop sign. Both were arrested because drugs were found in the car. New Jersey State law states that if drugs are found in a car and no one admits to ownership, everyone in the car is charged with possession. The officers found drugs on the woman so she got charged. The police did not search Ashley at the scene for some reason. After they got to the police station, Ashley figured they would search her anyway so she voluntarily surrendered the drugs and paraphernalia she had been hiding on her person. She figured it would be better for her to do so. Needless to say, she got charged too. Five charges to be exact. She was lucky that her father bailed her out of jail, but she was put on probation for five years. However, two years later, she had to go to court for a possible violation of probation.

The night before she had to go to court, I wrote Ashley a brilliant letter destroying every argument that probation could possibly come up with to violate her. I went into her room to hand it to her around midnight and she was as high as a kite. I thought to myself, "You've got to be kidding me." I felt like I wasted my time writing that letter.

She went to court early the next morning and tried to beat the urine test using clean urine from her sister but was still so high she messed it up. The official administering the test got suspicious and they swabbed her instead. She failed the drug test miserably. She was arrested immediately and incarcerated in the county jail.

I went to court with Ashley for her hearing to make sure she understood everything and didn't say anything harmful to her case. Her five charges carried a possible combined maximum sentence of fourteen years in prison and $140,000 in fines. Since this was Ashley's first brush with the law, her sentence was a choice of three years of imprisonment in the women's state prison and $14,000 in fines or five years of drug court. Ashley's family was pushing her to do drug court, but after hearing about drug court from other prisoners and noticing that people who were on drug court were back in jail within a month, she decided to take the three years in prison. The judge was surprised at her decision as he personally liked drug court and thought it worked. Ashley said she prayed about her decision and was at peace with it. She was fully prepared in her heart to serve those three years.

When the time came for her sentencing, her case was one of the last on the docket that day. The court session had ended before her case could be heard and Ashley was sent back to the prison. She wasn't too happy about it at the time as she wanted to get it done and over with. Little did we know then, but God was working behind the scenes. When she went back to court the following week, the judge who originally heard her case was on vacation and a different judge presided. The favor of God was on Ashley that day. The new judge only sentenced her to five months of imprisonment and a $3,000 fine.

Ashley toughed out her "wilderness moment," including detoxing cold turkey off of every illegal drug and prescription medication that was in her system at the time of her incarceration as well as nicotine. It was a tough two months for her as she was detoxing and she had to be rushed to medical a couple of times because of it. After her system was clean, she decided to finally straighten out her life. Since getting out of prison, she has done just that. She has made a miraculous turn around for the better, thanks to her faith in God, the birth of her second son and my steadfast friendship and positive influence. I am so proud of her!

## Paternity Issues

If the drug addicted individual has children, this can cause paternity issues involving the custody of their children. I have seen numerous addicts with children investigated by State Child Protective Services after being reported by an anonymous individual. If the accusations prove valid, Child Protective Services can force the individual to seek some sort of treatment, such as psychological counseling or drug rehabilitation, or risk losing custody of their children. I have seen both in my dealings with drug addicted individuals. Ashley lost custody of her eldest son when he was three-years-old because of her drug addiction. Custody was given to her son's father and, in her youthful naivety, she signed away all her parental rights. Years later, she admitted this was one of the dumbest things she ever did. Because of her drug addiction, she was only allowed supervised visits with her son. Ashley's story does have a happy ending though. Nine years after losing custody of her son, and after being clean for two years, she was able to go to court and get joint custody. She is an awesome mom now and I have to say, an even better parent than her son's father.

Another paternity issue is that the drug addicted individual can often be absent from their children's lives for an extended period of time. A few weeks after Ashley and I first met, I found out she had a son. She had never mentioned him in the previous few weeks and she admitted that she hadn't seen him in a while. I asked her, "How long has it been since you've seen him?" She responded, "Three months." I said, "Three months?! Go and see your son!" With my encouragement, she picked up the phone that night and called her son's father and asked how he was doing. She then made arrangements to visit him. Because of her addiction, Ashley would often go weeks or even months without seeing her son.

One of my cousins was a heroin addict and her sister told me when she was using, she would disappear for weeks. When she stopped using, she would come home to her husband and four children. Her addiction eventually led to divorce. I believe that her untimely death was because of a drug overdose, although I have never received confirmation of this.

**Moral Issues**

When a person is addicted to drugs, their moral compass is severely affected in a negative manner. Addicts will think nothing of stealing money or credit card information to pay for their drug habit, even from friends and family members. Like I said earlier, Ashley once stole $500 that her sister gave their father for their mother's tombstone. I have another friend who stole money that her father had earmarked for her nephew's medical device. I know someone who used to steal her boyfriend's tax return money every year. That money was supposed to be used to get his driver's license back so he could get a job and help support their three children. If the drug addict does have a legitimate job, they won't hesitate to steal from that job.

Women will use men to get money and material goods (food, clothing, cigarettes, etc.). This usually entails exchanging various sex acts. Sometimes, it is with a select group of friends and acquaintances, or it can develop into full blown prostitution. I have witnessed both in my interactions with drug addicted individuals. Sometimes, women will also work in strip clubs to make large sums of money quickly.

Addicts will think nothing of stealing prescription medication from friends and family. Often, the victims of these thefts are forced to buy their prescribed medication off the street in order to survive until their prescription renews. This causes an undue and unfair financial burden on the victims of the crime. The addict doesn't even care if it is another family member they are stealing prescription medication from, nor do they care that they are posing a serious health risk to their family member. All they care about is getting high.

Another moral issue drug addicts face is their lack of credibility. The number one rule that I've learned in dealing with people who are drug addicted is this, 'Drug addicts lie.' They will lie to hide their habit. They will lie as to why they need money. They will lie about why they don't want to hang out. And they will lie about their whereabouts (usually to use drugs, acquire money, come down from their last high, or detox off of medication they cannot acquire more of). They will even lie if they get caught in a lie or caught doing what they promised they wouldn't do anymore. In these situations, I'm reminded of my "Golden Rule of Developing Trust," which states:

*"Trust but verify."* – Ronald Reagan

Another golden rule that goes hand in hand with this one, the "Golden Rule of Maintaining Trust," is:

*"Trust and transparency go hand in hand."*

Drug addicts are master manipulators and will not hesitate to exploit someone's sympathy or empathy for their own selfish gain. They will tell the most convincing sob stories ever heard to make someone feel sorry for them. They will make a million promises that sound good, but they will deliver on none of them. They manipulate people, even loved ones, all in a quest to get what they want from them.

## Other Moral Issues

Another moral issue that was experienced by a family member of mine was that of physical abuse when her husband was high on cocaine. Not willing to put up with her husband's addiction and not wanting their two young daughters exposed to that, she divorced her husband and spent some time in a battered woman's shelter. She would go on to raise her daughters the best that she could as a single mother, which she was for the rest of her life.

# CHAPTER NINE

# FALSE HOPE AND SNEAKY ADDICTION

## Methadone – A False Hope

I have personally known numerous individuals who were taking Methadone to try and curb their addiction to opiates at one time or another. The concept of an opiate addict taking Methadone is similar to the concept of a smoker using a nicotine patch. The nicotine patch feeds the user's nicotine addiction without the harmful health issues that smoking tobacco products would cause. The same is true for Methadone users. Methadone feeds the user's opiate addiction without the effect of getting high. So, in essence, Methadone is the equivalent of a nicotine patch for opiate addicts.

While the concept of taking Methadone sounds good on paper, in practice, it is a less than desirable solution as it causes other issues which I have observed with my own eyes. One of the most common side effects is severe drowsiness. I have observed Methadone users come home after getting their daily dose and proceeding to sleep for the next three to five hours. I have even pulled more than one friend off the toilet after they passed out on it. Of course, when someone sleeps half the day, it is nearly impossible to find a job, not that they could hold onto one anyway. Almost all the Methadone users I have known were unemployed and not capable of holding a job. They usually had to "hustle" to make money, which often led to moral issues.

A Methadone user's whole life revolves around that Methadone clinic, whether it was traveling to get their daily dose of Methadone or to the required counseling sessions the clinics often required their patients to attend several times a week. I have a friend who once was contemplating whether to go on two-week vacation to the Caribbean with another friend of hers. My first reaction to her was, "Where are you going to get your daily Methadone dose from?" She hadn't thought about that and had no idea. I pointed out to her that she was basically a slave to Methadone because it affected every aspect of her life. Needless to say, she reluctantly decided not to take her friend up on the vacation offer because she could not go one day without Methadone, let alone two weeks.

One of the other negative aspects of Methadone is that it is highly addictive itself and takes twice as long to detox from than heroin. The Methadone user usually has to be slowly tapered off of it to minimize the excruciating pain and other negative side effects it often creates when a person is in withdrawal. I have seen this process take anywhere from six months to a year to complete. Often, the Methadone user halts the scheduled tapering rate because they can't bear the side effects. This prolongs the length of time it takes for them to completely detox. Unfortunately, I have seen Methadone users who were completely detoxed and went back to using heroin because they did not want to be a slave to Methadone again. In reality, Methadone does not deliver people from opiate addiction. It just substitutes one form of bondage, albeit a less deadly one, for another form of bondage.

Methadone also does nothing for individuals who abuse non-opiate drugs, such as cocaine, crack, methamphetamines, LSD, etc. I have known several individuals who were on Methadone but were still using non-opiate drugs. Methadone is not a cure-all, it's a crutch. It is not as effective as advertised.

51

## Xanax – The Sneaky Addiction

As discussed earlier, depression and anxiety can be a couple of reasons why people turn to drugs. Drug addiction can even exasperate these issues. Xanax is the brand name of the drug Alprazolam. It is in a drug class known as Benzodiazepine (or Benzo for short). While I know a few people who have been prescribed low doses and have no vulnerability to getting addicted to it, I have also known several drug addicted individuals who were prescribed Xanax by a physician, for anxiety in particular. However, being an addict, it wouldn't be long before the person would get addicted and abuse it. This would lead to the prescription running out before the next refill was available and the person would then be forced to buy it off the street to feed their addiction. The Xanax they bought off the street was usually a much higher dose than prescribed by most physicians. This then leads to other side effects, with the most common being sedation and memory loss.

I have known people who were addicted to Xanax who slept half the day away and one woman who passed out in the middle of receiving oral sex. The Xanax addicts I've known had a lot of trouble remembering things in general, even something as important as a doctor's appointment. Heck, one Xanax addict I knew would forget she took her prescription medication an hour later and would take it again. This caused all kinds of issues for her.

It is because of my experiences with Xanax addicts that I have a strong dislike for this medication. I often warn others who are taking it about how highly addictive it is and about its damaging side effects.

# CHAPTER TEN

# RULES FOR THOSE WHO
# INTERACT WITH DRUG ADDICTS

Several years ago, I came up with a set of rules for dealing with drug addicts. These rules served me well whenever I followed them. I hope they can serve others as well.

- Rule #1 – "Drug addicts lie."
- Rule #2 – "Drug addicts will do anything and say anything in order to get their next fix."
- Rule #3 – "Never give a drug addict cash or access to your credit/debit card."
- Rule #4 – "If an addict asks for money for a particular thing, offer to buy that thing for them. If they decline the offer, it reveals they really wanted the money for drugs."
- Rule #5 – "Never get romantically involved with a drug addict."

These rules are meant to protect others from being manipulated by an addict, not for people to be mean spirited toward the addict. Yes, the addict may become offended and mad at people for sticking to these rules. But it is in the mutual interest of both the individual and the addict to stand strong in their convictions regarding these rules.

## Explanation of These Rules

### Rule #1

I have explained this in part earlier, but it's suffice to say that drug addicts will not hesitate to lie if it serves their purpose.

### Rule #2

To a drug addict, getting their next fix is their number one priority and they don't care what they have to do in order to get it. If they have to lie, make up excuses, cheat, steal, prostitute, or take advantage of people (even their friends and loved ones), they will do it. They will say and do anything to get that next fix and they don't care if they hurt others in the process.

### Rule #3

The reason we should never give a drug addict cash or access to our credit/debit card is that they will most likely use it to purchase drugs. They will also abuse the card to meet other needs that they have. Drug addicts are typically broke and/or unemployed and are reliant on others for their needs beyond their drug habit. Necessities such as food, cigarettes, clothes, etc. are a struggle to finance so they will abuse the card if it's given to them.

I remember making this mistake in the past. I gave a friend my card so she could buy one summer outfit that she had begged me to buy for her as she didn't have any clothes that fit due to a recent large increase in weight gain. I grudgingly gave her my card as I worked a lot of hours at the time and wasn't able to take her myself. Not only did she buy an outfit, but she also bought more clothes for herself and her sister.

After she got home, she confessed that she "got a little out of control" and spent $200. I was furious because that was my bill money she had spent. At least she felt remorse when I told her that.

Another time, I had given another friend my card number because she was constantly asking me to order her food while I was at work. Because my job kept me busy, I gave her my card info so I wouldn't be burdened with ordering her food every day. Well, I soon found out that she didn't have an issue with how much she was spending on food. She had no problem spending $20-plus dollars on lunch every day. One day, I found a charge from Amazon Prime on my bank statement for a purchase I had not made. I was about to call Amazon about it when her cousin ratted her out. My friend admitted to making that unauthorized purchase and told her cousin not to tell me, like I wouldn't find out otherwise. When I confronted my friend about it, she admitted she had made the purchase and tried to justify it by saying, "Well, you would have bought it for me anyway." While that may have been true, it did not justify her action.

## Rule #4

As drug addicts tend to be broke and/or unemployed, they constantly ask people for money to support their drug habit, as well as other more legitimate needs like food, shelter, clothing, etc. In my experience, they will say they need the money for a legitimate reason, but more times than not, they need the money to support their drug habit.

After I came up with Rule #3, I decided a wiser course of action would be to offer to buy the addict the thing they requested the money for. More often than not, they declined my offer to purchase the item they supposedly needed. At first, I couldn't understand why they would refuse if they really needed that item. Usually they would say things like, "Nah, that's alright," "I don't want to inconvenience you," or some other lame excuse that didn't make any logical sense. It took me a while but I finally caught on to their scheme. They were lying to me and saying they wanted the money for a legitimate need when they really wanted the money to purchase drugs. Ever since then, when a drug addict requested money from me, I would ask them what they wanted it for. When they told me, I would offer to purchase that thing for them. If they declined my offer, I knew they really wanted the money to purchase drugs.

Because most drug addicts are practiced and habitually liars, they are very good at convincing people that their so-called "legitimate" need is actually legitimate. Being a very giving person and being the type of person who likes to believe the best in everyone, I cannot count how many times I got burned this way. It would often cost me way too much money before I finally caught on to their scheme.

## Rule #5

The reason we should never become romantically involved with a drug addict is because emotions tend to cloud our judgement. This is true for any romantic relationship as well. However, when we become romantically involved with a drug addict, our emotions for that person have a tendency to not only cloud our judgement but have greater consequences. We are more likely to enable the addict's addiction by giving them money and providing for their other needs which they usually don't have the means to acquire otherwise. In our heart, we want to help the other person but we are really just enabling them and making ourselves poorer in the process.

I made this mistake on several occasions. As long as the addict was willing to meet my selfish needs, I was willing to give the addict what they wanted, even though it bothered me to do so at times. It was a cycle that I found hard to break. It is hard to put aside the emotional factor when we see someone we care about suffering and we can do something about it. This doesn't only include romantic affiliations, but friendships as well. I have always had a very giving nature and had trouble saying "no" in these situations. Well, not being able to say "no" ended up costing me $8,000 and pretty much wiped me out financially and I dealt with the consequences of that poor decision for months.

Another reason we should not get romantically involved with a drug addict is because they will invariably use our emotions for them to their advantage. They will get us to give them the money they need to purchase drugs and persuade us to provide for their other needs as well, including material needs like food, clothing and cigarettes. They will also try to convince us to pay some or all their bills.

A friend of mine related her experience of dating a drug addict. Fortunately, she was able to get away from him, but not before he pulled her stepfather into his drama. After they broke up, she had been naive enough to think she could somehow help him get sober by offering to take his teenage daughter into her (and her stepfather's) home, so the addict could go to rehab. He never finished rehab, due to an injury, and ended up moving into the house with them, against her wishes...and the chaos ensued from there. That was the catalyst that introduced several more drug addicts into their lives.

My friend was able to move away from the situation, but her stepfather continued to help the addicts because he was charmed by a young female drug addict who arrived on the scene shortly after my friend moved out. She said that the crazy-busy stressful episodes never ended. There was always "something" dramatic going on in his or his daughter's life that put her and her family at risk emotionally, financially and physically. There was never peace or time for her own self-care. Even though my friend had broken up with her drug addict boyfriend after only a few months, that short relationship affected her and her stepfather financially for the rest of their lives. He and his friends continued to infiltrate their lives, long after the relationship ended. My friend warned that drug addicts can be as charming as Satan himself, luring people to destruction. She said that it messed her up mentally for a while and she started thinking about suicide, even though she had never been suicidal before.

The original drug addict soon introduced her stepfather to another 30-year-old female addict, who started sleeping with him to make him think she was his "girlfriend." For several months, she talked him into giving her as much money as she could. When he reached his generosity limit, she created a story to have him arrested on false charges of sexually molesting children. Within hours of his arrest, she took over his house and moved her *real* boyfriend in. She then convinced him to sign over Power of Attorney to her to manage his finances while he was in jail. Instead of handling his bills, she immediately went to work to empty his bank accounts, open credit cards in his name and max them all out, pull all cash-value out of his life insurance policy, steal everything of value in the house, and she gave his new paid-off truck to her boyfriend who crashed it in a DWI. The female addict plotted this whole scheme from the start. The total damage exceeded $350,000 within about a year of their initial introduction.

My friend's stepfather was a "mark" as her target because he was a naive alcoholic with an 8th grade education who blacked out frequently. He had no means to defend himself in court with his public defender. Fortunately, my friend was able to help him eventually get her out of his life, but not before he lost everything he had of value.

Another danger is that we may get sucked into using drugs as well. I have learned from my own experiences in other areas of my life that people tend to act like those they hang out with. This is why drug rehab facilities harp on incorporating the "people, places and things" theory into the addict's mental therapy counseling.

I once gave thought to using marijuana because one summer I was sharing a motel room with marijuana users who would have pot parties every weekend. Now, mind you, I have never taken drugs before or even contemplated it. However, there was one beautiful woman who participated in the pot parties that I kind of had a crush on. After a while, I considered trying marijuana as a means to get closer to her. I found out she went to a university that was only seven miles from where I lived and thought there was a possibility I could date her. However, she said something that turned me off. She said she would smoke every day if she had someone to smoke with. That was when I told myself it was not worth it. Fortunately, I never succumbed to trying pot, even when some of the others tried to peer pressure me into it.

In addition, I have seen the dangers of "casual" addicts dating more addicted individuals. "Casual" addicts claim they only use enough of the drug to "maintain" and function. However, when they dated the more addicted individual, their addiction got deeper than ever before and they did things they never did before, like shooting heroin instead of snorting it for example.

This rule is even more applicable for addicts who want to date other addicts. However, their addictions usually make each other worse as addicts tend to be broken individuals with unresolved trauma in their lives. A broken individual cannot fix another broken individual, no matter how kindhearted they might normally be outside of their addiction. One broken person plus one broken person does not equal two whole people. It equals two people who are more broken now that they are together than when they were apart. This is because the brokenness of the other person compounds their own brokenness. I witnessed this personally in the addicts I know.

# PART III: WHY ADDICTS STRUGGLE TO OVERCOME ADDICTION

## CHAPTER ELEVEN

## GENETIC PREDISPOSITION OR GENERATIONAL CURSE?

There is a debate, especially in Christian circles, whether drug addiction that seems to run in families is caused by genetic predisposition or is the result of a generational curse. Let's examine this debate.

**Genetic Predisposition**

Genetic predisposition is defined as "an increased chance or likelihood of developing a particular disease based on the presence of one or more genetic variants and/or a family history suggestive of an increased risk of the disease. Having a genetic predisposition does not mean an individual will develop the disease. Lifestyle and environmental factors can also affect an individual's risk of disease. Also called genetic susceptibility, hereditary predisposition, and inherited predisposition."[9]

---

[9] *National Cancer Institute,* "genetic predisposition," accessed November 2, 2024, at https://www.cancer.gov/publications/dictionaries/genetics-dictionary/def/genetic-predisposition.

Many people, especially those with a family history of addiction, are curious to know what factors play a role in addiction. Is addiction genetic?

According to American Addiction Centers,[10] it is true that some people may have a genetic predisposition to addiction, also known as a substance use disorder (SUD), a medical condition defined by the uncontrollable use of substances despite the negative consequences. However, having a genetic predisposition doesn't mean those individuals are guaranteed to develop an addiction. Genetics is just one of the many factors that can impact an individual's overall risk.

According to the National Institute on Drug Abuse,[11] family studies that include identical twins, fraternal twins, adoptees, and siblings suggest that as much as half of a person's risk of becoming addicted to nicotine, alcohol, or other drugs depends on his or her genetic makeup.

According to a study published by the University of Rutgers' Rutgers Addiction Research Center,[12] more than half of the differences in how likely people are to develop substance use problems stem from DNA differences, though it varies a little bit by substance. Research suggests alcohol addiction is about 50 percent heritable, while addiction to other drugs is as much as 70 percent heritable.

---

[10] Stacy Mosel, L.M.S.W., "Is Drug Addiction Genetic?," *American Addiction Centers*, (February 7, 2024), accessed November 2, 2024, at: https://americanaddictioncenters.org/rehab-guide/addiction-genetic.
[11] "Genetics and Epigenetics of Addiction," *National Institute on Drug Abuse*, (August 2019), accessed November 2, 2024, at: https://www.issup.net/files/2019-09/genetics_and_epigenetics_drugfacts_2.pdf
[12] "Rutgers Researchers Delve Deep Into the Genetics of Addiction," *Rutgers Institute for Translational Medicine and Science*, (November 9, 2022), accessed November 2, 2024, at: https://ritms.rutgers.edu/news/rutgers-researchers-delve-deep-into-the-genetics-of-addiction/.

According to the University of Utah's Learn Genetics Genetic Science Learning Center,[13] the A1 form (allele) of the dopamine receptor gene *DRD2* is more common in people addicted to alcohol, cocaine and opioids. The variation likely affects how drugs influence the reward pathway.

As we can see from the above, there does seem to be some scientific evidence to support genetic predisposition. However, my contention is that while genetic predisposition is genetically possible, it is just the physical manifestation of the actual root cause. This root cause is a generational curse. Let's examine this in more detail.

## Generational Curses

According to The Gospel Coalition, a "generational curse describes the cumulative effect on a person of things that their ancestors did, believed, or practiced in the past, and a consequence of an ancestor's actions, beliefs, and sins being passed down."[14] A generational curse is passed down from one generation to another, even if subsequent generations are not guilty of the things that initiated the curse.

One of the most famous generational curses found in the Bible is in Exodus 20:4-6. This is the second of the Ten Commandments that God gave to Moses on Mount Sinai. It states:

> *"You shall not make for yourself a carved image—any likeness of anything that is in heaven above, or that is in the earth beneath, or that is in the water under the earth; you shall*

---

[13] "Genes and Addiction," *University of Utah*, accessed November 2, 2024, at: https://learn.genetics.utah.edu/content/addiction/genes/.

[14] "How Generational Curses Affect My Love Life," *The Source*, (July 21, 2020), accessed November 2, 2024, at:
https://www.thesource.org/post/generational-curses-affect-my-love-life#:~:text=What%20is%20a%20Generational%20Curse,bound%20by%20th ese%20generational%20curses.

> *not bow down to them nor serve them. For I, the* LORD *your God, am a jealous God,* **visiting the iniquity of the fathers upon the children to the third and fourth generations of those who hate Me***, but showing mercy to thousands, to those who love Me and keep My commandments"* (Exodus 20:4-6).

We can see the generational curse attached to this Commandment in the bold text. This particular curse goes out four generations beyond the original violator. In other words, the original violator not only curses themselves, but they also curse their children, their grandchildren and their great-grandchildren. Three generations of that family will suffer from a curse they had no part in.

Some generational curses are perpetual until someone in the family line breaks them. These curses are prolonged because subsequent generations continue to practice the original violation, subsequent generations perpetuate the curse by their words (we will learn more about the power of words in a later chapter), or because a specific demon entered the family line through a particular violation.

There are three types of generational curses—casual, confessional and combined. Let's look at examples of each one.

## Causal Generational Curses

Causal generational curses are curses initiated through actions or choices. They are passed down from one generation to another, even if the succeeding generations are totally ignorant of its existence. Even Christians can be the victims of these curses. I know because I was. Unless the original curse gives a specific limit, causal generational curses will almost always continue indefinitely until they are broken.

This type of curse is usually broken by a member of the family in which the curse resides.

I found a causal generational curse in my family line after I started doing genealogy research on my family tree six years after my paternal grandmother passed away. My parents hadn't cleaned out her bedroom in our house. When I started doing my genealogical research, I went into my grandmother's bedroom and thoroughly went through her stuff. I found many precious treasures and records in her room. One thing I did not expect to find was her sister's business card from the Masonic lodge she belonged to. My grandmother's sister was a Freemason. I knew from experience that Freemasonry is a huge no-no. It is basically a false religion that secretly worships Satan, although their members don't find out until they reach the 33rd Degree.

As I continued my genealogical research online, I came across a website called Find-a-Grave that enabled people to find gravesites all over the country and usually contained photos of the tombstones. I found the tombstone pictures for my grandmother's immediate family and the Masonic symbol was on the tombstones of her parents, two sisters and two brothers. Additionally, one of her sisters-in-law had the symbol of the Order of the Eastern Star (a Masonic appendant body) on it. Once I found this out, I broke that generational curse in the name of Jesus.

## Confessional Generational Curses

Confessional generational curses are curses generated by individuals through the negative words they confess. This can be done either knowingly or unknowingly. Sometimes, people can curse themselves and other family members without even realizing it. The Bible says in Mark 11:23:

*"For assuredly, I say to you, whoever says to this mountain,*
*'Be removed and be cast into the sea,' and does not doubt in*
*his heart, but believes that those things he says will be done, he*
*will have whatever he says"* (Mark 11:23).

In other words, "You have what you say." This is why it is so vitally important to guard the words that come out of our mouth. Ever since Jesus defeated Satan at the cross, Satan doesn't have any real power. The only thing he can do is to trick people into manifesting their own destruction. He does this by influencing people to speak negative words against themselves. This is why we hear the words "death" and "killing" in so much of people's speech. Phrases such as, "My back is killing me," "My knees are killing me," "You'll be the death of me," and "I laughed so hard I thought I was going to die."

Confessional generational curses will continue until they are broken. Once the curse is broken, the previous negative confession should be replaced by a positive confession regarding that same situation. Phrases like, "By His stripes I am healed," "No weapon formed against me shall prosper," and "I laughed so hard I cried tears of joy."

When I was growing up, I would on occasion hear my father say, "The Pohl men don't live past sixty-five." I didn't think much of this statement at the time. However, by the time I was forty-five, my view on that statement changed. I was a mature Christian and had a lot of knowledge about curses. When I heard my father utter that curse, I said to myself, "You're not putting that on me!" I had no intention of dying in twenty years. In fact, I always confessed that I planned on living the full one hundred and twenty years the Bible told me I was entitled to, which was based on the common misconception of Genesis 6:3 which states:

*"And the LORD said, 'My Spirit shall not strive with man
forever, for he is indeed flesh; yet his days shall be one hundred
and twenty years'"* (Genesis 6:3).

I soon broke the curse my father uttered in the name of
Jesus! I do not believe my father intentionally tried to
perpetuate a curse on subsequent generation of men in the
Pohl family. I do believe that his "belief" in this matter was
based on his recent family history. His father died at the age
of sixty-four. His paternal uncle died at the age of sixty-seven.
His brother died at the age of sixty-six. His paternal
grandfather died at the age of forty. This does not quite line
up with his confession, but I believe it is based on the fact
than none of his five maternal uncles lived past the age of
sixty-five.

It was several years after I had broken that curse when I
started to see the results. My father did not die before the age
of sixty-five, though he did slow down a bit at sixty-five.
When my father was in his early eighties, he said to me one
day, "I didn't expect to live this long. I have no idea how I
have lived this long." I simply replied to him, "You're
welcome!" I then told him how I had broken that curse years
ago because I did not want that placed on me. I'm not sure if
he understood what I said at that time, but my father lived
until exactly one month before his eighty-fourth birthday,
when he was ready in his heart to die and chose to leave this
earth of his own free will.

## Combined Generational Curses

A combined generational curse is rarer than the previous
two types of curses. It is a combination of both a causal and
a confessional generational curse. A good example of this
type of curse is found in the Bible in Matthew 27. When
Pontius Pilate tried to free Jesus because he found no fault in

him, he gave the people the choice to free either Jesus or Barabbas. The Scripture tells us:

> *"Now at the feast the governor was accustomed to releasing to the multitude one prisoner whom they wished. And at that time they had a notorious prisoner called Barabbas. Therefore, when they had gathered together, Pilate said to them, 'Whom do you want me to release to you? Barabbas, or Jesus who is called Christ?' For he knew that they had handed Him over because of envy. While he was sitting on the judgment seat, his wife sent to him, saying, 'Have nothing to do with that just Man, for I have suffered many things today in a dream because of Him.' But the chief priests and elders persuaded the multitudes that they should ask for Barabbas and destroy Jesus. The governor answered and said to them, 'Which of the two do you want me to release to you?' They said, 'Barabbas!' Pilate said to them, 'What then shall I do with Jesus who is called Christ?' They all said to him, 'Let Him be crucified!' Then the governor said, 'Why, what evil has He done?' But they cried out all the more, saying, 'Let Him be crucified!' When Pilate saw that he could not prevail at all, but rather that a tumult was rising, he took water and washed his hands before the multitude, saying, 'I am innocent of the blood of this just Person. You see to it.' And all the people answered and said, 'His blood be on us and on our children.' Then he released Barabbas to them; and when he had scourged Jesus, he delivered Him to be crucified"* (Matthew 27:15-26).

The key verse in this passage of Scripture is verse 25: "And all the people answered and said, 'His blood be on us and on our children.'" This is the verse that initiated the combined generational curse on the Jewish people. I believe that curse is why the Jewish people have been persecuted throughout the centuries ever since. Not only were they guilty of rejecting their Messiah, but they initiated a combined generational curse through their confession. Look at the suffering of the Jewish people since then.

The Romans sacked Judea in 70 A.D., tore down their temple and scattered the Jewish people throughout the Roman Empire in what would become known as the Great Jewish Diaspora. It is because of this diaspora a great many Jews could be found in Europe in the coming centuries. This would eventually lead to other great persecutions such as the Spanish Inquisition and the Holocaust. The nation of Israel had to fight for its very existence in three wars against its Arab neighbors in which she was severely outnumbered. Even today, Israel's enemies have sworn to wipe them from the face of the earth. Iranian leaders have even sworn that as soon as they develop an atomic bomb, they will drop it on Israel, despite knowing it will mean their own nuclear destruction. The Jewish people have paid a heavy price indeed because of that combined generational curse uttered nearly 2,000 years ago!

## My Conclusion

It is my firm belief that so-called "genetic predisposition" is really a physical manifestation of a generational curse, which is spiritual by nature. Generational curses manifest in the natural as genetic anomalies, which cause all kinds of physical and mental health woes. These genetic anomalies are then passed down to subsequent generations. To learn how to break generational curses, see chapter fifteen.

# CHAPTER TWELVE

# DRUGS AND DEMONS

## The Unknown Spiritual Aspect

The biggest and most important aspect of drug addiction is unknown to most people. This is the spiritual aspect and implications of drug addiction. These ignorant individuals even include those professionals tasked with helping drug addicts to deal with and recover from their addiction. People are often led to believe that addiction is a disease, which is a lie.

The prevalent view amongst both medical and mental health professionals worldwide is that drug addiction is a disease. This view is held by prestigious organizations such as the American Medical Association (AMA), the National Institute on Drug Abuse (NIDA), the Substance Abuse and Mental Health Services Administration (SAMHSA), and the National Institutes of Health (NIH). A great many psychologists hold this view as well.

According to the National Institute on Drug Abuse:

"Addiction is a chronic, often relapsing brain disease that causes compulsive drug seeking and use, despite harmful consequences to the addicted individual and to those around him or her."[15]

---

[15] *National Institute on Drug Abuse,* "Drugs, Brains, and Behavior: The Science of Addiction Drug Misuse and Addiction," accessed December 8, 2024, at https://nida.nih.gov/publications/drugs-brains-behavior-science-addiction/drug-misuse-addiction.

Addicts are made to believe they are diseased and that this disease is incurable. They are told it can only be managed through rehab, meetings, medication, and therapy. All the while, the real underlying cause is often ignored, either willfully or through complete ignorance.

While drugs do have an effect on one's brain and body, drug addiction is NOT a disease. People who believe it is a disease believe this because they can only see the addiction in the natural, physical realm. Most are totally unaware of the spiritual component of drug addiction and I believe that God has given me this revelation to share with others.

The reason why drug addicted individuals seemingly can't stop using drugs despite their negative consequences is because drug addiction is really a spiritual yoke of bondage. What do I mean by a "yoke of bondage?" Bondage implies slavery or slavish thinking. A yoke is the instrument or means of enslaving someone or something. Drug addicts are victims of this spiritual yoke of bondage.

The spirits responsible for placing this yoke of bondage on people are demons. No amount of medication, rehabilitation, psychotherapy, or incarceration can truly deliver a person from this yoke of bondage because it is spiritual, not physical. Jesus tells us who is ultimately responsible for putting yokes of bondage on people.

*"So ought not this woman, being a daughter of Abraham, whom Satan hath bound—think of it—for eighteen years, be loosed from this bond on the Sabbath?"* (Luke 13:16).

This Scripture teaches us that it is Satan (and his demon cohorts) who put yokes of bondage on people. The Bible often lumps Satan and his demonic underlings together when describing their work.

People who use drugs can often become victims of these demons and get trapped in a spiritual yoke of bondage. While they may not start out with intending to become victims, the enemy gradually ensnares them in this yoke. I have a friend who is currently trapped in one. In fact, she is trapped in a continuous cycle of being clean for a few weeks, using again for a few weeks, and back to being clean again for a few weeks. No matter how much effort she puts into trying to stay clean, she inevitably slips back into using drugs. This just verifies she is trapped in a spiritual yoke of bondage because the program she keeps attending has not had much effect in helping her overcome her drug addiction.

While I do not discourage rehabilitation or psychotherapy, they are just bandaging a much deeper problem that requires a more permanent solution. It's like putting a bandage on a stab wound. It is merely a temporary patch that keeps a person stabilized until a more permanent solution can be undertaken.

The Bible is very clear when teaching the reader who is the One who delivers people from spiritual yokes of bondage.

*"I am the LORD your God, who brought you out of the land of Egypt, that you should not be their slaves; I have broken the bands of your yoke and made you walk upright"*
(Leviticus 26:13).

*"For it shall come to pass in that day,' Says the LORD of hosts, 'That I will break his yoke from your neck, And will burst your bonds; Foreigners shall no more enslave them"*
(Jeremiah 30:8).

*"It shall come to pass in that day That his burden will be taken away from your shoulder, And his yoke from your neck, And the yoke will be destroyed because of the anointing oil"*
(Isaiah 10:27).

*"Then the trees of the field shall yield their fruit, and the earth shall yield her increase. They shall be safe in their land; and they shall know that I am the LORD, when I have broken the bands of their yoke and delivered them from the hand of those who enslaved them"* (Ezekiel 34:27).

## Original Spiritual Reasons for Drug Usage

The original spiritual reason for most drug usage was as a part of pagan, demonic or satanic worship. African witch doctors, Celtic and Native American shamans, the participants of the Native American practices of vision quests and contacting spirit animals, the practitioners of Voodoo, and those who worshiped demons and even Satan himself take drugs in order to contact the spirit realm. This is because drugs are a short cut into seeing into the spirit realm. Just ask anyone who has had an LSD or PCP trip. When they say they are "hallucinating," they are really seeing into the spirit realm and they are seeing demons!

Several years ago, Ashley was given cocaine that was laced with PCP by a so-called "friend." The effects on her were not only as advertised on drug related websites but a major side effect was the "hallucinations," both audio and visual.

At first, they seemed harmless and even comical. While she was being supervised by her sister and brother-in-law, she was watching a movie with them. In this movie, a man was raping a woman and Ashley yelled out, "Now that's a real man!" Ashley's niece, who was in the room at the time, was appalled by this statement and admonished Ashley for it. That phrase would soon become her catchphrase for the week. She said it to her nephew's stuffed animal. She said one time when she was in the shower. As I walked into the bathroom, she uttered her now infamous phrase. I initially took that as a complement aimed at me, but then she said, "Okay, I love you. Bye-bye," as if she was talking to someone on the phone. However, the next day it became more serious.

Ashley tried to leave the house and walk to her son's house that whole day, which was five miles away and across a major highway. I had to physically prevent her from leaving the house several times. That evening, I consulted with her sister, Marie, and we both agreed we needed to call Adult Protective Services (APS) because Ashley required 24-hour supervision given her condition. We were afraid she would leave the house while I was sleeping, attempt to walk to her son's house and get hit by a car trying to cross that highway. Luckily, she went with the APS people voluntarily because she thought the ambulance driver was cute. Subsequently, she was taken to the psychiatric unit of our local hospital for evaluation and possible treatment.

After my first visit with her, I noticed Ashley was staring at the wall and ceiling most of the time I was there, even when I was talking to her. She claimed her neck was "stuck." I had to tell her to look at me to break her gaze from the wall or ceiling. She had a look of fear on her face as she gazed at what she was seeing. After observing this behavior, I asked her what she was looking at. I asked her to describe it to me in detail. After she did, I could tell the PCP in her system had broken the spiritual plane and she was seeing into the spiritual realm. She saw demons everywhere.

By the third day, I began to think Ashley had done permanent brain damage to herself. Before I departed for the evening, she had a moment of clarity and asked me to pray for her and I did. I rebuked the demons, asked the Holy Spirit to purge her system of all drugs, and asked God to heal her mind.

The next day, she was scheduled to be transferred to a long-term psychiatric facility. She had already been held at the hospital past the 72-hour maximum period they were allowed to keep her. I went to visit the next day with Marie, just as Ashley had requested the night before. I had some paperwork that I needed to give to the nurse as well. As I went into the psychiatric unit, I was greeted by Ashley who didn't have a happy look on her face. In fact, she was mad because she had been put there by Marie and I. I told Ashley I needed to give the paperwork to the nurse, but she insisted I give it to her instead and she would give it to the nurse. I didn't want to do that because I didn't trust Ashley in the frame of mind she had been in for the previous week. We went back and forth a few times and finally she said angrily, "Just give me the damn paperwork and send Marie in!" I said to myself, "Yup, she's back to normal." Thank God my prayers for her the night before had been answered and she had snapped out of it sometime between the two visits. She was cleared for release by the doctors shortly thereafter and we went home later that day. Ashley had been high for a week before she was delivered. That is one experience I do not ever want to relive again.

Ashley's ordeal was a result of illegal drug use, but the spiritual plane can be broken by other kinds of drugs too. A few years before my mother died, she was in the hospital for a couple of weeks. They had her so doped up on medication that she claimed on more than one occasion she was seeing "black smoke" in the corners of the ceiling in her hospital room. I didn't realize it at the time, but she was seeing demons. I didn't make that connection until much later after seeing an episode of the television series "Supernatural" where it showed a demon, in the form of black smoke, exiting the mouth of a demon possessed man who was delivered from that demon.

I witnessed this black smoke firsthand myself, many years later. I saw that black smoke exit my mouth after I cast out the demon in the name of Jesus, just like I had seen it in that television series.

## What is a Demon?

A demon is an evil spiritual entity. Demons are the disembodied spirits of the Nephilim. The Nephilim were the giant, hybrid offspring of fallen angels (called "Watchers" in the Book of Enoch) and human women, which can be seen in the Book of Genesis.

> *"There were giants on the earth in those days, and also afterward, when the sons of God came in to the daughters of men and they bore children to them. Those were the mighty men who were of old, men of renown"* (Genesis 6:4).

We can see God's judgement against the giants in the Book of Enoch:

> *"And now, the giants, who are produced from the spirits and flesh, shall be called evil spirits upon the earth, and on the earth shall be their dwelling. Evil spirits have proceeded from their bodies; because they are born from men, [and] from the holy Watchers is their beginning and primal origin; [they shall be evil spirits on earth, and] evil spirits shall they be called. [As for the spirits of heaven, in heaven shall be their dwelling, but as for the spirits of the earth which were born upon the earth, on the earth shall be their dwelling.] And the spirits of the giants afflict, oppress, destroy, attack, do battle, and work destruction on the earth, and cause trouble: they take no food, [but nevertheless hunger] and thirst, and cause offences. And these spirits shall rise up against the children of men and against the women, because they have proceeded [from them]"*
> (Enoch 15:8-11).[16]

---

[16] *The Book of Enoch*, by R.H. Charles, [1917], accessed October 28, 2024, at: https://sacred-texts.com/bib/boe/boe018.htm.

This is why these evil spirits, called demons, seek to ultimately possess someone. It is because they lost the ability to experience the physical pleasures and sensations they once had before they were disembodied. They were born as physical beings and long to live like that again.

When a person uses drugs, it gives demons a legal doorway into their life and the right to put the yoke of drug addiction around their neck, even if they are saved. There is a reason marijuana is called "The Gateway Drug." Most believe it is called this because its users often try harder drugs like cocaine or heroin, which possibly leads people to become addicted to them. A lot of times this can be true. However, marijuana is often the key that opens a spiritual gateway that demons use to first enter in a person's life when they start taking drugs.

Back in the New Testament era, drugs and witchcraft were so synonymous with one another that the same Greek word, "pharmakeia," was used for both in the original texts. It's where we get our modern English word "pharmacy" from. According to Strong's Exhaustive Concordance of the Bible (5331), "pharmakeia" means "medication" and is often translated as "sorcery" and "witchcraft" in older translations of the New Testament. It was believed that when a person took drugs, they were participating in witchcraft. Even in the modern-day practices of hardcore Satanism, the practitioners call themselves witches and warlocks. While the higher up ones have direct contact with demons, the lower-level ones use drugs to contact the spiritual realm (demons) during their ceremonies. Anyone who has ever read the Bible in depth would know that witchcraft is strongly condemned throughout.

Demons can oppress the body through pain and disease. They can oppress the soul (mind, will and emotions) through various means including fear, depression, grief, anxiety, loneliness, suicidal thoughts, and various so-called "psychiatric issues." These "psychiatric issues" include bi-polar disorder, multiple personality disorder, incest, and pedophilia. Of course, demonic oppression also includes all forms of addiction (drugs, alcohol, gambling, etc.).

Demons can be destroyed. Jesus taught us that:

> *"The thief does not come except to steal, and to kill, and to destroy. I have come that they may have life, and that they may have it more abundantly"* (John 10:10).

The Apostle Peter adds to this when he said:

> *"Be sober, be vigilant; because your adversary the devil walks about like a roaring lion, seeking whom he may devour. Resist him, steadfast in the faith, knowing that the same sufferings are experienced by your brotherhood in the world"*
> (1 Peter 5:8-9).

The goal of demons is to steal our joy, happiness and peace. They want to destroy our finances, relationships, mental health, and physical health. Their ultimate goal is to kill us and send us to Hell where they can torture us for all of eternity. Drug addiction happens to be one of their more powerful methods of accomplishing these goals, but it can be overcome as we will see.

The demonic spirit of addiction that torments drug addicted individuals often does not come alone when they enter a person's life. They usually bring subordinate demonic spirits with it. They will bring psychological demonic spirits such as depression, anxiety and bipolarism to mentally torment the individual. Addiction will bring carnal demonic spirits such as fornication, adultery and prostitution. Addiction will also bring financial demonic spirits such as theft and exploitation (causing the addict to use others for selfish gain). Addiction brings these carnal and financial demonic spirits with it in order to facilitate the acquisition of drugs.

Not only does the spirit of addiction want to enslave people, but its ultimate goal is to kill them. In order to accomplish this task, addiction brings its powerful buddy, the demonic spirit of death, later on after the individual has become a slave to their addiction. This demonic spirit of death empowers the lower-level spirits that addiction brought along with it. The spirit of death uses these newly empowered spirits to exponentially increase their effectiveness in an individual's life. An individual will be more likely to succumb to the lower-level spirits' influence and be swayed to kill themselves, knowingly or unknowingly. Their primary way of doing this is by influencing the individual to overdose on drugs.

I have witnessed this effect on someone I know who intentionally overdosed twice in a 24-hour period in an attempt to commit suicide because she was severely depressed. Thank God her sister was home and saved her life on both occasions. This same individual later admitted to me that she had overdosed two more times while away from home. Fortunately, the paramedics were able to save her life both times. This individual was told each time she overdosed that she was dead. By the grace of God, she not only survived all four overdose attempts, but she did not suffer any negative health issues as a result. I told her, "I don't know what God has planned for you, but it must be something pretty spectacular considering how hard the devil was trying to kill you."

# PART IV: DELIVERANCE

## CHAPTER THIRTEEN

## THE REAL ANSWER TO OUR PROBLEMS

### Deliverance of an Unsaved Individual

Jesus taught us what happens in the spirit realm when a demon is cast out of a non-saved person. We can see His teaching in the Gospel of Luke:

> *"When an unclean spirit goes out of a man, he goes through dry places, seeking rest; and finding none, he says, 'I will return to my house from which I came.' And when he comes, he finds it swept and put in order. Then he goes and takes with him seven other spirits more wicked than himself, and they enter and dwell there; and the last state of that man is worse than the first"* (Luke 11:24-26).

This is why it is paramount for a non-saved person who has been delivered from demons to accept Jesus Christ as their Lord and Savior after getting delivered. Not doing so can result in a person being much worse off later than he originally was to begin with.

### Deliverance of a Saved Individual

We can see an example of this during Jesus' earthly ministry in His dealing with the individual commonly referred to in Christian circles as "The Madman of Gadara." Modern mental health professionals would have diagnosed him as having "multiple personality disorder." As we will see from the Scripture, his condition was not a psychiatric issue, but a demonic one.

*"Then they sailed to the country of the Gadarenes, which is opposite Galilee. And when He stepped out on the land, there met Him a certain man from the city who had demons for a long time. And he wore no clothes, nor did he live in a house but in the tombs. When he saw Jesus, he cried out, fell down before Him, and with a loud voice said, 'What have I to do with You, Jesus, Son of the Most High God? I beg You, do not torment me! For He had commanded the unclean spirit to come out of the man. For it had often seized him, and he was kept under guard, bound with chains and shackles; and he brake the bonds and was driven by the demon into the wilderness. Jesus asked him, saying, 'What is your name?' And he said, 'Legion,' because many demons had entered him. And they begged Him that He would not command them to go out into the abyss. Now a herd of many swine feeding there on the mountain. So they begged Him that He would permit them to enter them. And He permitted them. Then the demons went out of the man and entered the swine, and the herd ran violently down a steep place into the lake and drowned. When those who fed them saw what had happened, they fled and told it in the city and in the country. Then they went out to see what had happened, and came to Jesus, and found the man from whom the demons had departed, sitting at the feet of Jesus, clothed and in his right mind. And they were afraid. They also who had seen it told them by what means he who had been demon-possessed was healed. Then the whole multitude of the surrounding region of the Gadarenes asked Him to depart from them, for they were seized with great fear. And He got*

*into the boat and returned. Now the man from whom the*
*demons had departed begged Him that he might be with Him.*
*But Jesus sent him away, saying, 'Return to your own house,*
*and tell what great things God has done for you.' And he went*
*his way and proclaimed throughout the whole city what great*
*things Jesus had done for him"* (Luke 8:26-39).

As we can see from the above Scripture passage, not only did the man get delivered of the demons that possessed him, but immediately afterward, he decided to follow Jesus. Jesus then commissioned him to go back to his hometown to be a witness to what had happened to him and he went on to evangelize his city. He went from being a victim of demon possession to being an evangelist. What a tremendous turnaround!

## Can a Saved Christian Have Demons?

This is a controversial topic that is debated in Christian circles. Can a saved Christian have demons? Based on my own personal experiences and observations, the answer would be a resounding yes! If a person had demons inside of them before they were saved, the demons are still present after they are saved. While demons would not have the ability to possess them, because the Holy Spirit now resides in their spirit, they can still oppress the individual's body and soul (mind, will and emotions).

I know three individuals who got saved but were still plagued by their addiction for a year or more afterwards. When I cast that demon out of myself, as mentioned in an earlier chapter, I had been saved for twenty-four years. However, being saved, the demons were easier to cast out in the name of Jesus without the repercussions that non-saved individuals are open to.

## Why Drug Addicted Individuals Need Deliverance

The reason drug addicts need deliverance even if they are saved is because of that spiritual yoke of bondage mentioned earlier. Being saved won't destroy that yoke, only deliverance will.

I have a friend who passed away as the result of a heroin overdose about a month after she accepted Jesus. I have another friend who accepted Jesus at the same time back in 2018 and she still struggles with her drug addiction to this day. A person can be saved but not delivered.

## Jesus: The Real Answer to Our Problems

The Apostle Peter wrote in his Epistle to the Hebrews:

*"Seeing then that we have a great High Priest who has passed through the heavens, Jesus the Son of God, let us hold fast our confession. For we do not have a High Priest who cannot sympathize with our weaknesses, but was in all points tempted as we are, yet without sin. Let us therefore come boldly to the throne of grace, that we may obtain mercy and find grace to help in time of need"* (Hebrews 4:14-16).

Jesus understands our weaknesses and our struggles. He greatly desires for us to come to Him for deliverance from not only our sin, but also all those things that Satan and his demon cohorts are plaguing us with, including the yoke of drug addiction. Kenneth Copeland once said, "Jesus doesn't have the answer, He IS the answer, and the answer to everything is a manifestation of His anointing."

## What is the Anointing?

The Old Testament prophet Isaiah wrote:

*"It shall come to pass in that day. That his burden will be taken away from your shoulder, And his yoke from your neck, And the yoke will be destroyed because of the anointing oil"*
(Isaiah 10:27).

It is the Anointing that will destroy the yoke of drug addiction in a person's life, once and for all. The Anointing is the burden removing, yoke destroying power of God. It's God on flesh doing those things that flesh can't do, doing the so-called "impossible." All throughout the Gospels and the Book of Acts are many accounts of Jesus and His followers healing and delivering people using the Anointing.

This testimony told by the Apostle Mark is an example of the Anointing for healing:

*"Now a certain woman had a flow of blood for twelve years, and had suffered many things from many physicians. She had spent all that she had and was no better, but rather grew worse. When she heard about Jesus, she came behind Him in the crowd and touched His garment. For she said, 'If only I may touch His clothes, I shall be made well.' Immediately the fountain of her blood was dried up, and she felt in her body that she was healed of the affliction. And Jesus, immediately knowing in Himself that power had gone out of Him, turned around in the crowd and said, 'Who touched My clothes?' But His disciples said to Him, 'You see the multitude thronging You, and You say, 'Who touched Me?' And He looked around to see her who had done this thing. But the woman, fearing and trembling, knowing what had happened to her, came and fell down before Him and told Him the whole truth. And He said to her, 'Daughter, your faith has made you well. Go in peace, and be healed of your affliction"*
(Mark 5:25-34).

The power that flowed out of Jesus to the woman was the Anointing.

Another example can be read in the early Acts of the Apostles:

> *"And through the hands of the apostles many signs and wonders were done among the people. And they were all with one accord in Solomon's porch. Yet none of the rest dared join them, but the people esteemed them highly. And believers were increasingly added to the Lord, multitudes of both men and women, so that they brought the sick out into the streets and laid them on beds and couches, that at least the shadow of Peter passing by might fall on some of them. Also a multitude gathered from the surrounding cities to Jerusalem, bringing sick people and those who were tormented by unclean spirits, and they were all healed"* (Acts 5:12-16).

The unclean spirits mentioned in verse 16, and throughout the New Testament for that matter, are demons. The "shadow of Peter" is a reference telling us that the Anointing was so strong on the Apostle Peter that it would radiate outward to a distance equivalent to the length of his shadow.

**The Word of God Contains the Answer**

In the Gospel of John, we read concerning Jesus:

> *"In the beginning was the Word, and the Word was with God, and the Word was God. He was in the beginning with God. All things were made through Him, and without Him nothing was made that was made. In Him was life, and the life was the light of men. And the light shines in the darkness, and the darkness did not comprehended it...And the Word*

> *became flesh and dwelt among us, and we beheld His glory,*
> *the glory as of the only begotten of the Father, full of*
> *grace and truth"* (John 1:1-5,14).

In this Scripture passage, John teaches us that Jesus is the living incarnation of the Word of God (the Word made flesh). Jesus Himself has this to say about the Word of God:

> *"It is the Spirit who gives life; the flesh profits nothing. The*
> *words that I speak to you are spirit, and they are life"*
> (John 6:63).

The Apostle Peter adds to this witness in his Epistle to the Hebrews when he wrote:

> *"For the word of God is living and powerful, and sharper than*
> *any two-edged sword, piercing even to the division of soul and*
> *spirit, and of joints and marrow, and is a discerner of the*
> *thoughts and intents of the heart"* (Hebrews 4:12).

Therefore, the written Word of God is not just words written by men, as the world believes. It is alive and it is just as powerful and has as much authority behind it as if Jesus Himself was speaking it.

# PART V: HEALING

## CHAPTER FOURTEEN

## WHAT DOES THE WORD OF GOD SAY ABOUT COMMON PROBLEMS?

As stated earlier in this book, drug addicted individuals suffer from many issues that result from their addiction or may have caused an individual to start using drugs. Let us examine what the Word of God has to say about them.

**The Word of God Concerning Depression**

During a troubling time in his life, King David of Israel was suffering from depression, but he also knew how to get out of it. In the following Scripture we can see his self-conversation:

> *"Why are you cast down, O my soul? And why are you disquieted within me? Hope in God; For I shall yet praise Him, The help of my countenance and my God"*
> (Psalm 42:11).

Being a musician and the author of many of the Psalms, David knew from experience that praise and worship defeats depression. Why is this? It is because the Word of God says that God inhabits the praises of His people:

> *"But You are holy, Enthroned in the praises of Israel"*
> (Psalm 22:3).

The Word of God also says that in the presence of God is the fullness of joy:

> *"You will show me the path of life; In Your presence is fullness of joy; At Your right hand are pleasures forevermore"*
> (Psalm 16:11).

When we praise and worship God, it draws the presence of God, in the person of the Holy Spirit, and it brings the fullness of joy.

I remember years ago when I was at my job and, for some unknown reason, I started to feel the spirit of depression come on me. I had enough wisdom at the time to recognize this and knew what to do about it. I started singing every praise and worship song I knew and in about 30 minutes, that spirit left me. Praise be to God!

## The Word of God Concerning Anxiety

Anxiety is a common yoke of bandage that afflicts many people today and doctors are all too eager to treat it with medication. The most common medicine prescribed is Xanax. However, this medication is highly addictive and has many negative side effects, including memory loss, loss of balance (which can lead to injury), and sedation (which can make operating a vehicle dangerous). All the Xanax addicts I know are unable to function properly for even 12 hours. Most sleep half the day away, can't remember important things like doctor appointments, and can't handle other important responsibilities, such as caring for their children. Of course, they are unable to hold a job either. Most Xanax addicts will eventually buy it off the street as they quickly build up a tolerance to the drug. It causes financial distress for them which in turn can lead to amoral behavior to acquire the funds to pay for their addiction. The Word of God tells us the answer for anxiety:

> *"Be anxious for nothing; but in everything by prayer and supplication, with thanksgiving, let your requests be made known to God; and the peace of God, which surpasses all understanding, will guard your hearts and minds through Christ Jesus"* (Philippians 4:6-7).

When we pray to God about our problems and believe Him for the solutions, it brings peace to both our heart and our mind. While we are waiting for God's provision, the enemy will try to tempt us into thinking negatively about our situation. This is why the Word of God continues on from the previous passage and tells us what we should fill our minds with instead of worries and doubts:

> *"Finally, brethren, whatever things are true, whatever things are noble, whatever things are just, whatever things are pure, whatever things are lovely, whatever things are of good report, if there is any virtue and if there is anything praiseworthy— meditate on these things"* (Philippians 4:8).

## The Word of God Concerning Grief

Grief can be a crippling emotion. I have a friend who lost her mom five years ago and is still not over it. While her dad has healed from the loss and has started dating again, she vehemently disapproves of him dating anyone and doesn't want her father's new girlfriend anywhere near her. It's as if she considers her father dating the equivalent of him cheating on his wife. In another incidence, I once dated a woman who visited her father's grave every day for a year after he passed

89

away. Neither situation is healthy. The Word of God contains promises to those suffering from grief:

> *"He heals the brokenhearted And binds up their wounds"*
> (Psalm 147:3).

> *"To console those who mourn in Zion, To give them beauty for ashes, The oil of joy for mourning, The garment of praise for the spirit of heaviness; That they may be called trees of righteousness, The planting of the LORD, that He may be glorified"* (Isaiah 61:3).

> *"Blessed are those who mourn, For they shall be comforted"*
> (Matthew 5:4).

> *"...Blessed are you who weep now, For you shall laugh"*
> (Luke 6:21).

## The Word of God Concerning Peer Pressure

The Word of God teaches us to not be conformed to the world and its views and beliefs:

> *"And do not be conformed to this world, but be transformed by the renewing of your mind, that you may prove what is that good and acceptable and perfect will of God"* (Romans 12:2).

Often, especially in this day and age, the world's view and beliefs are in direct conflict with the Word of God. This can make it so much harder to go against the flow of the world. If we do, we will often be ridiculed as being a nut job, a religious fanatic, a racist, a bigot, a homophobe, or any of a myriad of other derogatory labels. The only thing the Word of God teaches us to conform to is the image of Jesus.

*"For whom He foreknew, He also predestined to be conformed
to the image of His Son, that He might be the firstborn among
many brethren"* (Romans 8:29).

The Word of God also warns us about the dangers of peer
pressure when it states:

*"Do not be deceived: 'Evil company corrupts good habits'"*
(1 Corinthians 15:33).

## Get Rid of Stinkin' Thinkin'

One of the most important things we must do is to rid
ourselves of our old way of thinking and renew our mind with
the Word of God. The Word of God says:

*"And do not be conformed to this world, but be transformed by
the renewing of your mind, that you may prove what is that
good and acceptable and perfect will of God"* (Romans 12:2).

The Word of God also tells us in Ephesians 5:26 that Jesus
cleanses us by "…the washing of water by the word." Our
mind needs to be brainwashed! When most people think of
brainwashing they think of psychological brainwashing,
which is done by nefarious individuals for sinister purposes.
Various government agencies (the CIA with "MK Ultra" in
particular), Hollywood, social media, and the traditional
mainstream media outlets have been guilty of this type of
brainwashing in recent years. However, renewing our mind
by the washing of the water of the Word of God is
brainwashing, but in a good way. It is a spiritual brainwashing.
It will help us to renew our mind to think like God thinks and
act like Jesus acted during His earthly ministry.

Here is why this is important. The Word of God in
Genesis 1:26 tells us that God made man in His image and

according to His likeness. One of these ways in which man is created in God's image is that we are triune (3-in-1) beings. God is a triune being: Father, Son and Holy Spirit. Man is also a triune being: spirit, soul (mind, will and emotions) and body. When it comes to our spirit, soul and body, two-thirds majority rules. Whichever two-thirds are dominate, that is the way we will go. This is important to know because 90 percent of the battles in life take place in our mind and this is where the enemy will attack us most often. So, whichever one our mind is aligned with, that is the way we will go. By default, our mind will align with our flesh (body). If that remains so, we will go the way of the world and be vulnerable to the enemy's attacks. However, if we renew our mind with the Word of God, it will align with our spirit and we will go God's way. From this, we can receive healing, deliverance and peace amongst others benefits. The Apostle Paul exhorts us to put away old thinking and to renew our mind when he wrote:

*"This I say, therefore, and testify in the Lord, that you should no longer walk the rest of the Gentiles walk, in the futility of their mind, having their understanding darkened, being alienated from the life of God, because of the ignorance that is in them, because of the blindness of their heart; who, being past feeling, have given themselves over to lewdness, to work all uncleanness with greediness. But you have not so learned Christ, if indeed you have heard Him and have been taught by Him, as the truth is in Jesus: that you put off, concerning your former conduct, the old man which grows corrupt according to the deceitful lusts, and be renewed in the spirit of your mind, and that you put on the new man which was created according to God, in true righteousness and holiness"*
(Ephesians 4:17-24).

Please note, this battle can be very difficult at times because the enemy will do everything in its power to make us falter. Even the Apostle Paul, the man who wrote two-thirds of the New Testament, tells us about his own struggles between his spirit, soul and body. He wrote:

> *"For I know that nothing good dwells in me, that is, in my flesh. For I have the desire to do what is right, but not the ability to carry it out. For I do not do the good I want, but the evil I do not want is what I keep on doing. Now if I do what I do not want, it is no longer I who do it, but sin that dwells within me. So I find it to be a law that when I want to do right, evil lies close at hand. For I delight in the law of God, in my inner being, but I see in my members another law waging war against the law of my mind and making me captive to the law of sin that dwells in my members. Wretched man that I am! Who will deliver me from this body of death? Thanks be to God through Jesus Christ our Lord! So then, I myself serve the law of God with my mind, but with my flesh I serve the law of sin"* (Romans 7:18-25 ESV).

Another important reason it is vitally important to change our old mindset is as the Word of God says regarding a man:

> *"For as he thinks in his heart, so is he…"* (Proverbs 23:7).

We need to rid ourselves of all negative thoughts concerning ourselves and our situation. Never speak negative confessions such as:

- "I can't do it."
- "I'll never overcome this."
- "I would be better off dead."

Instead, we should be confessing what the Word of God says about us, if we are born-again that is. The Word of God says about the believer:

> *"Yet in all these things we are more than conquerors through Him who loved us"* (Roman 8:37).

Instead of thinking those negative and worldly thoughts, the Word of God tells us what kind of thoughts to meditate on in Philippians 4:8—whatever things are true, noble, just, pure, lovely, of good report, and anything that is virtuous and praiseworthy.

The Word of God also tells us that believers have world overcoming power. Jesus told us:

> *"These things I have spoken to you, that in Me you may have peace. In the world you will have tribulation; but be of good cheer, I have overcome the world"* (John 16:33).

In addition, the Word of God tells us:

> *"Most assuredly, I say to you, he who believes in Me, the works that I do he will do also; and greater works than these he will do, because I go to My Father"* (John 14:12).

In combination, these two Scriptures tell us that we have the same world overcoming power that Jesus Himself has! We just have to believe in Him and believe we are world overcomers.

## The Word of God Concerning Unforgiveness

Unforgiveness is a "poison pill" that many victims of trauma are adversely affected by. It is like taking poison and expecting the other person to die. Unforgiveness does not affect the person we won't forgive; it only affects us!

The Bible tells us about the dangers of unforgiveness in Hebrews 12:

> *"Pursue peace with all people, and holiness, without which no one will see the Lord: looking carefully lest anyone fall short of the grace of God; lest any root of bitterness springing up cause trouble, and by this many become defiled;"*
> (Hebrews 12:14-15).

In Matthew 6, we learn that if a person does not forgive those who have wronged them, they themselves will not be forgiven by God:

> *"For if you forgive men their trespasses, your heavenly Father will also forgive you. But if you do not forgive men their trespasses, neither will your Father forgive your trespasses"*
> (Matthew 6:14-15).

I know two individuals who were raped by their grandfather when they were young children. Obviously, they were traumatized by these incidents. Even after their grandfather went to prison, served his time and gave his life to Jesus while imprisoned, they never forgave him. They would get angry with their father, who had forgiven him and would hang out with his father. They would still refer to him as "that rapist" even after he came to Christ. I tried to teach one of the individuals about redemption and that the person her grandfather is now in Christ is not the same person who raped her when she was a child. Despite my best efforts, she stubbornly refused to listen and let go of her unforgiveness. She then told me that she couldn't wait for him to die (he was 92 at the time) so she could urinate and defecate on his grave.

My mother held unforgiveness toward her three brothers ever since the death of their father. I've heard two different stories concerning what happened between them. At the time of their father's death in 1977, the story I heard was that they accused my mother of manipulating their father to changing his Will so she would inherit everything. This was not so. My grandfather was illiterate his whole life. He could not read or write. His signature was literally just an "X." My mother assisted him with his banking, amongst other things, so her name was on his account. She got deeply offended by their accusation and never spoke to any of her brothers ever again. Many years later, one of them tried to reconcile but she would have none of it.

The second story was told by my father shortly before his passing in 2018. He said that my mother had every intention of dividing their father's money evenly between the four of them, but her brothers wanted more. I don't know which story is factual, but I can see my grandfather willing to leave my mother everything in his Will. She took him in and he lived with us for the last eight years of his life. When he was on his deathbed, my mother took care of him. All during the time my grandfather was suffering from cancer, not one of his three sons came to visit him, not even once. However, when it came time to read the Will, they were right there.

## Unforgiveness Ruins Physical Health

This root of Unforgiveness ruins the physical health of people. My friend suffered from many health ailments for many years as a result of her stubborn refusal to forgive her grandfather and died at the age of forty-two. My mother also suffered a great deal from poor health, especially in the last ten years of her life, due to her refusal to forgive her brothers. She died at the age of seventy-two.

## Redemption

The Bible tells us about redemption in the following scriptures:

> *"'Come now, and let us reason together,' Says the LORD, 'Though your sins are like scarlet, They shall be as white as snow; Though they are red like crimson, They shall be as wool"* (Isaiah 1:18).

> *"I, even I, am He who blots out your transgressions for My own sake; And I will not remember your sins"* (Isaiah 43:25).

> *"In Him we have redemption through His blood, the forgiveness of sins, according to the riches of His grace"* (Ephesians 1:7).

> *"Therefore, if anyone is in Christ, he is a new creation; old things have passed away; behold, all things have become new"* (2 Corinthians 5:17).

The Apostle Paul walked in this last Scripture when he wrote to the church in Corinth and said:

> *"Open your hearts to us. We have wronged no one, we have corrupted no one, we have cheated no one"* (2 Corinthians 7:2).

Paul could say this because after he met Jesus on the road to Damascus (Acts 9:1-9), he was changed forever just like the rest of the above Scripture stated. The sins he was guilty of when he was known as Saul of Tarsus (Acts 8:1-3) were null and void in God's eyes. Paul would later own up to his past and not run from it. He said during his defense in Jerusalem:

*"Brethren and fathers, hear my defense before you now.' And when they heard that he spoke to them in the Hebrew language, they kept all the more silent. Then he said: 'I am indeed a Jew, born in Tarsus of Cilicia, but brought up in this city at the feet of Gamaliel, taught according to the strictness of our fathers' law, and was zealous toward God as you all are today. I persecuted this Way to the death, binding and delivering into prisons both men and women, as also the high priest bears me witness, and all the council of the elders, from whom I also received letters to the brethren, and went to Damascus to bring in chains even those who were there to Jerusalem to be punished"* (Acts 22:1-5).

Just because a person has a "past" doesn't mean they have to be labeled by that past for the rest of their life. If they have accepted Jesus as their Lord and Savior, that "past" no longer exists, even though they, and others, may still have a memory of it.

# CHAPTER FIFTEEN

# NEXT STEPS

## Be Born-Again (Saved)

In the Gospel of John, Jesus has a conversation with a Pharisee named Nicodemus. The Pharisees were the Jewish religious leaders during Jesus' earthly ministry. Nicodemus wished to learn more about the Kingdom of God from Jesus so he sought him out.

> *"There was a man of the Pharisees named Nicodemus, a ruler of the Jews. This man came to Jesus by night and said to Him, 'Rabbi, we know that You are a teacher come from God: for no man can do these signs that You do unless God is with him.' Jesus answered and said to him, 'Most assuredly, I say to you, unless one is born again, he cannot see the kingdom of God.' Nicodemus said to Him, 'How can a man be born when he is old? Can he enter a second time into his mother's womb and be born?' Jesus answered, 'Most assuredly, I say to you, unless one is born of water and the Spirit, he cannot enter the kingdom of God. That which is born of the flesh is flesh, and that which is born of the Spirit is spirit. Do not marvel that I said to you, 'You must be born again.' The wind blows where it wishes, and you hear the sound of it, but cannot tell where it comes from and where it goes. So is everyone who is born of the Spirit.' Nicodemus answered and said to Him, 'How can these things be?' Jesus answered and said to him, 'Are you a teacher of Israel, and do not know these things? Most assuredly, I say to you, We speak what We know and*

*testify what We have seen, and we do not receive Our witness. If I have told you earthly things and you do not believe, how will you believe if I tell you heavenly things? No one has ascended to heaven but He who came down from heaven, that is, the Son of Man who is in heaven. And as Moses lifted up the serpent in the wilderness, even so must the Son of Man be lifted up, that whoever believes in Him should not perish but have eternal life. For God so loved the world that He gave His only begotten Son, that whoever believes in Him should not perish but have everlasting life. For God did not send His Son into the world to condemn the world, but that the world through Him might be saved. He who believes in Him is not condemned; but he who does not believe is condemned already, because he has not believed in the name of the only begotten Son of God. And this is the condemnation, that light has come into the world, and men loved darkness rather than light, because their deeds were evil. For everyone practicing evil hates the light and does not come to the light, lest his deeds should be exposed. But he who does the truth comes to the light, that his deeds may be clearly seen, that they have been done in God"*
(John 3:1-21).

The Apostle Paul teaches us how to get born-again when he wrote in his Epistle to the Romans:

*"that if you confess with your mouth the Lord Jesus and believe in your heart that God has raised Him from the dead, you will be saved. For with the heart one believes unto righteousness, and with the mouth confession is made unto salvation"*
(Romans 10:9-10).

### Prayer of Salvation

To be born-again, you must pray the prayer of salvation. Raise your hands to Heaven and confess this prayer out loud:

"I now confess with my mouth that Jesus is my Lord and believe in my heart that God raised Him from the dead. Lord Jesus, I repent of all my sins and ask that You wash them away with the holy, precious sinless blood of Jesus. Lord Jesus, come into my heart. Fill me with Your Holy Spirit. I thank You for this Father and give You all the praise and honor and glory for my salvation in Jesus' name, Amen!"

## Power and Authority Over the Enemy

As a believer, you have power and authority over demons in the name of Jesus. Jesus said:

*"Behold, I give you the authority to trample on serpents and scorpions, and over all the power of the enemy, and nothing shall by any means hurt you"* (Luke 10:19).

*"And these signs will follow those who believe: In My name they will cast out demons; they will speak with new tongues; they will take up serpents; and if they drink anything deadly, it will by no means hurt them; they will lay hands on the sick, and they will recover"* (Mark 16:17-18).

The Apostle James adds in his Epistle:

*"Therefore submit to God. Resist the devil and he will flee from you"* (James 4:7).

The Apostle Paul teaches us concerning the power of the name of Jesus:

*"Therefore God also has highly exalted Him and given Him a name which is above every name, that at the name of Jesus every knee should bow, of those in heaven, and of those on earth, and of those under the earth, and that every tongue*

*should confess that Jesus Christ is Lord, to the*
*glory of God the Father"* (Philippians 2:9-11).

The Old Testament prophet Isaiah prophesied concerning yokes of bondage:

*"It shall come to pass in that day, That his burden will be*
*taken away from your shoulder, And his yoke from your neck,*
*And the yoke will be destroyed because of the anointing oil"*
(Isaiah 10:27).

Once you are born-again, you now have the spiritual authority, in the name of Jesus, to cast out demons and destroy their yokes of bondage.

## Prayer for Deliverance

Raise your hand to Heaven and confess this prayer out loud:

"Dear Heavenly Father, I come to You in the name of Jesus. I repent of the sin of drug use and all other related sins. I ask that You wash them away in the holy, precious, sinless blood of Jesus. I declare that, in the name of Jesus, I am delivered from the yoke of drug addiction once and for all, for the yoke is destroyed because of the anointing. In the name of Jesus, I break any and all curses in my life and I break all generational curses that have affected me and my family. In the name of Jesus, I cast out any and all demons within me and cancel all demonic assignments against me. Holy Spirit, I ask that You purge my body of any and all drugs, both legal and illegal, that shouldn't be there, and heal my whole body and my whole soul. I ask for these, Father, giving You all the praise and honor and glory for them, believing I receive them, in Jesus' name. Amen!"

## Break Generational Curses

In order to break generational curses, you must do several things:

- You must recognize the existence of the curse.
- You must be willing to break the curse, even if you are not the one responsible for initiating it.
- You must remove any cursed objects from your home. Burn the objects if possible.
- You must repent on behalf of those in your generational line who are responsible for initiating and actively perpetuating the curse.
- You must declare the curse is broken in the name of Jesus and also declare that the curses' effects are null and void from this point forward.

## Follow-Up

Even after you are born-again and completely delivered from the yoke of drug addiction, the enemy will still tempt you into falling back into that old habit from time to time. When those thoughts arise, you must reject them and cast them down in the name of Jesus. The Word of God says concerning this:

> *"casting down arguments and every high thing that exalts itself against the knowledge of God, bringing every thought into captivity to the obedience of Christ,"* (2 Corinthians 10:5).

Do not dwell and mediate on the enemy's thoughts. You control your thoughts and align them with the Word of God as it is written:

> *"Finally, brethren, whatever things are true, whatever things are noble, whatever things are just, whatever things are pure, whatever things are lovely, whatever things are of good report, if there is any virtue and if there is anything praiseworthy— meditate on these things"* (Philippians 4:8).

When you find yourself in situations that feed the temptation, you must do what the Word of God says:

> *"Depart from evil, and do good; And dwell forevermore"* (Psalm 37:27).

> *"Flee also youthful lusts; but pursue righteousness, faith, love, peace with those who call on the Lord out of a pure heart"* (2 Timothy 2:22).

> *"Abstain from every from of evil"* (1 Thessalonians 5:22).

In addition, read your Bible and pray to God daily. Find yourself a good Bible-based, Spirit-filled church that preaches the uncompromised Word of God, attend regularly, get involved, and seek discipleship. All of this will help you grow as a Christian.

## The Power of Positive Confessions

If you are not careful, your speech will default to old habits and confessions. In other words, you will unconsciously confess what already exists or what you don't want anymore. You must confess the desired end result, even if you are not there yet.

Too many times, I have heard addicts confess they are addicts, even after they have overcome addiction. I have even heard of recovery programs that refer to addicts as if they will always be an addict for the rest of their life and the addiction can only be managed. Both attitudes are completely wrong! This only serves to reinforce what already exists. If you want a different outcome for your life, you need a different attitude and confession. For example, an addict could confess something like this:

> "I am grateful that I am no longer an addict and that old habits related to my past addiction are no longer a part of my life. I am creating new, positive habits that will help keep me clean once and for all. These new habits will help me to reach my full potential now that I no longer have drug addiction holding me back."

## My Prayer for the Reader

I hope this book has been both a revelation and a blessing to you. This is my earnest, heart-filled prayer for every reader of this book:

> "Dear Heavenly Father, I come to You in the name of Jesus. I ask that You grant revelation and knowledge to each and every reader of this book concerning drug addiction and the true answer to their problems. Give them the wisdom as to how to apply this to their lives and give them the strength and diligence to persevere in their journey towards deliverance and sobriety. I ask that You deliver them from any and all temptations that the enemy may bring to them. I ask that You remove all the people from their lives who are negative influences on them and replace them with people who will be a positive influence. I pray for complete healing

in their bodies and their souls, for by Your stripes they were healed. In the name of Jesus, I rebuke every demon and every demonic stronghold in their lives and cancel out every demonic assignment against them. In the name of Jesus, I break every curse that inflicts them and their families and declare that the yoke of drug addiction in their lives is destroyed once and for all, for the yoke is destroyed because of the anointing. I ask for all of these and give You all the praise and honor and glory and thanksgiving for them, believing I receive each and every one of them in Jesus' name, Amen!"

May the Lord bless you and keep you always. God bless each and every one of you!

# TESTIMONIALS

*"And they overcame him by the blood of the Lamb and by the word of their testimony..."* (Revelation 12:11).

*"...By the mouth of two or three witnesses every word shall be established"* (2 Corinthians 13:1).

The following stories are testimonies to the delivering power of God over drug addiction. If these individuals could overcome drug addiction once and for all, anyone can. I hope their testimonies will be an inspiration for others.

DISCLAIMER: All testimonials in this appendix were shared with me personally, shared in a public setting in which I heard them firsthand or were publicly shared on the Internet.

## Shawn Michaels – WWE Hall of Famer[17]

World Wrestling Entertainment (WWE) Hall of Famer Shawn Michaels has publicly related his testimony on how and why he came to the Lord in numerous interviews. During Shawn's first tenure with the WWE (1988-1998), he learned that he could pretend to be another person. He was nineteen-years-old at the time he joined the WWE and said he didn't even know what being a man was. He gained fame and notoriety as a professional wrestler in no time. He used to delude himself by saying, "I only party on the road." However, he was on the road up to 250 days a year. He said

---

[17] "Shawn Michaels Testimony." *YouTube,* uploaded by Vertical Church Films, January 3, 2017, https://www.youtube.com/watch?v=nsquMO7QreU.

he could let things come out in the ring honestly through drugs and alcohol. He said it was the only way he could show any type of personality other than the shy, quiet kid he really was. Over time, his WWE persona and who he really was sort of melded into one. He said, "I didn't know where Shawn Hickenbottom (his real name) ended and Shawn Michaels began."

In 1999, during his first retirement due to injury, Shawn was introduced to Rebecca Curci, and within a month they got married. Three months after marrying his wife, Shawn learned that she was pregnant and figured he had nine months to clean up his act but realized he still didn't have the ability to become this man he needed to become. In the meantime, his wife, who had grown up as a Christian, was plugged into a local church Bible study and developed a strong faith in Christ.

One weekend, Shawn said he got into a little bit of a haze and said his two-year-old son crawled on his chest and said, "Daddy's tired." Even at the age of two, his son could see the difference in his father and it hit Shawn like a ton of bricks. He realized it had been two plus years and he still had not cleaned up his act.

One day, he found himself at a local church. Feeling the draw of the Holy Spirit, he walked inside the church and told a lady inside that he was looking for a Bible study. Although she reacted oddly to his request, a man popped his head out of his office and said Shawn could come to his Bible study. The gentleman told him that if he wanted to be a part of this Bible study, he would have to accept Jesus Christ as his Lord and Savior and then asked Shawn if he would like that. Shawn replied, "You know something, I think I would." He said the sinner's prayer and then wept like a baby. They discipled him and he said that his life has never been the same and he has never touched another drug!

Since then, Shawn has not been shy about expressing his faith during his numerous cameos in the WWE since retiring from full-time wrestling. After retiring from wrestling for good in 2010, Shawn even appeared in the faith-based movie "The Resurrection of Gavin Stone."

## Demi Lovato – Singer/Actress[18]

Demi Lovato is perhaps most well-known for her early work with Disney, but her early life was a turbulent one. Lovato struggled with cocaine, alcohol and other drugs. Her addictions were exacerbated by vulnerabilities including bipolar disorder, a recurring eating disorder and high stress. Because mental illness greatly increases the risk of drug addiction, Lovato's case is much like millions of lesser-known people who turn to substances to cope with the symptoms of their disorder.

Her first sobriety lasted five years, followed by a near-death experience and drug overdose. Lovato turned to God and attended rehab. She stayed in a 12-Step sober home for three days a week and publicly attended 12-Step meetings. Lovato publicly attributes her recovery to God. She said, "I just feel like God gave me a voice, not just to sing with. He put me through those things, which seemed horrible at the time, but they were so worth it. With the obstacles I've overcome, I can help people."

## Martin Sheen – Actor[18]

Martin Sheen has been in the public eye for decades. He's beloved in roles like "Grace and Frankie," "Apocalypse Now," and the "Departed," and he's the famous father of

---

[18] *Christian Drug Rehab,* "Addicted Celebrities Who Turned to Christ," accessed December 8, 2024, at https://christiansdrugrehab.com/blog/addicted-celebrities-who-turned-to-christ/.

fellow actor Charlie Sheen. Like many in the public eye, Sheen eventually struggled with addiction and substance abuse. Sheen eventually developed an alcohol use disorder, culminating in a public breakdown and estrangement from his sons. Martin Sheen moved into rehab and re-found his faith, attending Alcoholics Anonymous. Today, Sheen has been sober for over a decade. He dedicates his time to the 12-Step Foundation, to volunteer efforts in his hometown of Los Angeles, and to other humanitarian efforts. Sheen attributes his salvation to God and to his ability to give back, which he feels helps him redeem himself and to see himself in the light of someone who is worthy of God.

## Kelsey Grammar – Actor[18]

This famous actor from the television series "Frasier" and "Cheers" didn't have the lighthearted life like his characters on TV. The death of his sister, father and two half-brothers led him to abuse drugs and alcohol. His drinking got so bad that he even served jail time for driving while intoxicated. He credits parts of his recovery to his faith in God stating, "As a Christian, we always fail because we can't become Christ. But I can try to at least emulate the best qualities, even if I may fall short."

## Pastor John J. Wagner – Epic Church International (Sayreville, NJ)

In his testimony to his congregation on Easter Sunday 2018, Pastor John J. Wagner related that he came to the Lord on Easter Sunday 1984. He said that he had finally broken down and came to church after a friend had been asking him for weeks. At the time he got saved, he said that he was "a drug addicted, drug dealing, twenty-year-old punk of a kid." While he was not delivered from drug addiction right away after getting saved, he eventually did. Thirty-four years later, he became the pastor of the largest church in the State of New Jersey. Pastor Wagner is living proof that God can use anyone, even a drug addicted individual, to have a positive effect on the Kingdom of God.

## Bishop Dr. Perry L. Austin – W.O.W Gospel Ministries International (Suffolk, VA)

Bishop Austin had a rough upbringing. He was born and raised in the hood of Bridgeport, CT by his beloved grandmother after his mother gave him up. He had a failed marriage in his early adult life and was estranged from his daughter from that marriage for decades. Bishop Austin has publicly admitted that, at one point in his life, he was addicted to crack. His addiction resulted in a period of homelessness for him and his family. It also nearly cost him his second marriage. One day, his wife gave him an ultimatum, "Us or the drugs!"

Fortunately, Bishop Austin made the wise choice and chose his family. He set aside the drugs and through the power of God was completely delivered from his addiction. Today, he is the founder and pastor of W.O.W. Gospel Ministries International (WGMI), which has led the revolution of online church, even before COVID hit. Many of the disciples he has made and nurtured through his ministry have gone on to form their own independent ministries. Bishop Austin is the founder of Leverage Academy of Leadership (Suffolk, VA) and is the President of XIXI Now Success Academy Worldwide (Montgomery, AL). He is also a certified John Maxwell Leadership Coach. Talk about a tremendous turnaround! If God can do it for him, he can certainly do it for anyone else.

# ABOUT THE AUTHOR

Thomas W. Pohl is the founder of War for Truth Ministries (wftministries.org) and has been ministering to drug addicts since 2015, mostly on a one-on-one basis. While he did not know it at the time, God was training him up for his calling to minister to drug addicts and those who love them. This calling was revealed to him in 2024 and God has since called him to expand his ministry to a wider audience. This book is one of the first steps in that expansion.

In 2018, after a dear friend died of a drug overdose, Thomas cried out to God in the midst of his pain and said, "Don't let her death be in vain, turn this around for good!" Four months later, after God had healed his heart from her loss, God answered his plea and dropped this book on his heart.

In addition to his ministry, Thomas is the founder and owner of Orange Knight Media (orangeknightmedia.com), the home of all non-faith-based media products created by Thomas, as well as the services he offers to clients. He is also the founder and owner of Cybervision Web (cybervisionweb.net), a company specializing in the design of websites for small businesses and non-profits.

On a more personal level, Thomas is a veteran of the United States Navy and his interests include military weapon systems, history, genealogy, sports, and science fiction. He receives great joy from spending quality time with his beloved godson Collin, whom he considers to be the son he never had.

www.ingramcontent.com/pod-product-compliance
Lightning Source LLC
Chambersburg PA
CBHW070755120626
46557CB00002B/602